Crosscurrents / MODERN CRITIQUES

Harry T. Moore, *General Editor*

Charles Shapiro

Theodore Dreiser:

OUR BITTER PATRIOT

WITH A PREFACE BY

Harry T. Moore

SOUTHERN ILLINOIS UNIVERSITY PRESS
Carbondale and Edwardsville

FEFFER & SIMONS, INC.
London and Amsterdam

In discussing Theodore Dreiser, I find that Charles Shapiro is a hard man to precede because he seems in his book to have said virtually everything that can be said about Dreiser now—at least about the man's works. My own contribution will be some general observations along with a few reminiscences; the latter won't have the value of an actual memoir, for they deal with Dreiser only from a distance, as a man seen but not talked with. So here goes.

I can remember Dreiser at a Hollywood party in the early 1930s. He may have been a little high, for he insisted upon calling everyone George—not a felicitous memory to have of so remarkable an author as Dreiser really was. The other remembrance is a happier and more significant one, of Dreiser a year or so before that lecturing in Mandel Hall at the University of Chicago. Perhaps he was no Robert Ingersoll or William Jennings Bryan on the platform, but the way he said what he said had great force.

Most of it may be found in his autobiographical volumes; he spoke to us largely of his newspaper days in Chicago, St. Louis, Toledo, Pittsburgh, and New York. In each place, he said, he found evils that the very newspapers he was working for wanted to keep covered up. He soon found that he could hastily fake a harmless "human-interest" story, which was what his editors wanted, and could spend the valuable hours of the day in the public library, going through Balzac and Darwin.

Dreiser read to us the words of a poster which had been sent to Europe to lure mill workers to Pittsburgh, words which promised them a land of milk and honey. He then described the labor conditions in the Pittsburgh factories, and of the squalid and sooty "homes" the men went to after their overlong hours before the coke ovens. In childhood I had seen some of this, purely from the outside, though by that time conditions had improved at least somewhat—but I began to understand much more about such matters as Dreiser webbed together, in this talk, the vileness that existed in city after city, all of it encouraged by the politicians and connived at by the so-called professional men. As I say, Dreiser put all this together for those of us who listened, gave it a pattern that helped us to understand better the hugeness of the evil—and this is what, at certain levels, Dreiser's novels do, although in some of them he seems to be caught in the same power machine that produced and perpetuated the evil itself.

Certainly Dreiser was an intellectually confused man, particularly in those last years of his life; but at least, in that one lecture at Chicago, he was clear and powerful, and he made his point with more force than I find it made in his autobiographical volumes. Those of us who attended the lectures at Mandel Hall in those days owe much to the Americans who spoke there—including the jesting, pessimistic Clarence Darrow and the chanting, optimistic Carl Sandburg, each of them continually brushing the cowlick out of his eye—for they made different aspects of our country real to us. Sandburg, Darrow, and Dreiser, three Midwestern men who pronounced their r-sounds as if their tongues were nutcrackers—they were natives of that Midwestern soil who looked as if they couldn't be fooled, though alas, in his later years Dreiser seemed to be, at times. He apparently couldn't make up his mind about Hitler, for like so many Americans of German ancestry, Dreiser was evidently impressed by the first real unifying of that ebullient nation Bismarck had created; and, after all, Hitler built gleaming roads and provided cheap cars for the people.

Dreiser, as if to balance his foolishness about Nazi Germany, also spoke well, toward the last, of Soviet Russia; but then, so did many other American writers in the 1930s and 40s. Dreiser, however, seems to be the only American author one might call major who took a Communist-party card. This was in the last months of his life, and both he and the Communists must have known better; at least Dreiser soon sounded off to the effect that he would sound off about anything he pleased, whenever he pleased—which would ultimately have caused embarrassment. But he was a dying man, unappreciated as the important novelist he was; the foolish acceptance of that membership card was perhaps a gesture of defeat as well as defiance. In any event, he made arrangements to be buried in what he called the most beautiful place he had ever seen, that fantastic and most un-Communist cemetery, Forest Lawn, which Evelyn Waugh made fun of so richly and so nastily. It's hard to think of Dreiser becoming a "loved one" there.

He died in 1945; he had been born in 1871 in Terre Haute, Indiana, and much of his youth was an escape from his family's Catholicism and from Terre Haute itself. But there was always in him nostalgia for Indiana and candle lights gleaming among the sycamores—

his brother was a writer of popular songs under the name of Paul Dresser, and Theodore wrote most of the words for Paul's famous tune, "On the Banks of the Wabash."

That was in his early New York period, which became an almost life-long residence that included an extended stay on skid row and years of success as the editor of slick magazines who wore a pince nez. Dreiser wrote his first novel, Sister Carrie—and it was as good as anything he ever did later—at the turn of the century, but couldn't get it properly published for seven years; and this wasn't his only brush with censorship. His troubles didn't arise out of erotic scenes, but rather out of the fact that his books gave sex, like wealth, the emphasis it actually had in American life.

But now let's let Mr. Shapiro take over. He has, I think, written a very fine critical study of Dreiser, and although he is never blind to his subject's faults, he writes of them in a way which accents the true importance of the man. Perhaps Mr. Shapiro is wrong about the Cowperwood trilogy in underplaying The Titan: I'm with H. L. Mencken in finding this novel better than its predecessor, The Financier. But Mr. Shapiro makes out a good critical case for what he says, as he does throughout his book. One of its great virtues is the way in which it demonstrates, really demonstrates, that each of Dreiser's novels is a deliberate artistic production emphasizing an important phase of our national life.

Mencken once said that he had spent forty years, without success, in trying to smooth out Dreiser's manner of writing. But it couldn't be done. Its very crudeness matches the crudeness of its subject matter, the vulgar, brash, strong, cruel, and yet somehow wonderful, even magnificent expansion of America. Mr. Shapiro deals with all these matters expertly, and he will now begin—let me say once again that I think he's a very fine all-round critic of this author who was himself some kind of a titan.

Harry T. Moore

August 2, 1962

Note

For eight years Mr. Shapiro's fine book has continued to sell, and now it is good to see it going into still another edition. As Dreiser's reputation as a writer has steadily improved, the present volume has consistently proved to be a valuable guide to his work.

H. T. M.

Southern Illinois University
December 1969

CONTENTS

THEODORE DREISER'S seemingly sprawling novels have, too often, been dismissed as inartistic, sociological documents. This study is an attempt to understand all of Dreiser's novels in terms of underlying themes which serve as foundations for each book. By viewing the novels as whole, unified entities rather than as awkward collections of paragraphs, I hope to demonstrate that Dreiser was an artist with a purpose, a writer who conceived and executed his work as a result of that purpose. Seeing America as a country emerging from its youth, he was concerned about a culture which was creating within itself goals which perverted the worthwhile institutions of the society and robbed the individuals of the chance to live up to their full, inherent potentialities.

Each of Dreiser's novels illustrates a different aspect of this crucial misdirection of America's energies. *Sister Carrie,* his first novel, concerns itself with a close study of the individual. It takes several protagonists from varied economic strata of American life and shows how they are harmed and corrupted by the fraudulant claims of a spurious American dream.

Jennie Gerhardt carries on this theme of misdirection, but the primary concern is now with the American family. Two families, polar opposites on the social scale, are presented; each is seen to crumble and fail. As in *Sister Carrie*, the blame falls on America, for the individual members of each family are shown to be decent, capable people. In his trilogy (*The Financier, The Stoic,* and *The Titan*) Dreiser, by concentrating on the career of a successful businessman, broadens the application of his thesis.

In *The "Genius,"* Dreiser tries to portray and understand the American artist. His basic theme this time is the study of the forces harmful to our creativity. Again, we have an organized, well-constructed novel, for the plot and characterization all tend to re-emphasize the basic action which is at the heart of the saga of the gifted, maladjusted artist. In my analysis of *The "Genius,"* I also hope to show deficiencies within the book which are due to a failure to clearly understand his subject.

The Bulwark is Dreiser's most unusual novel; yet it too can be seen in terms of the underlying action. Religion, after all, has often been hailed as the philosophical answer to our materialistic ambitions. Dreiser plots his novel around a good, believing Quaker, and tries to show what happens when moral scruples collide with American reality. Solon Barnes' struggle becomes tragic as we realize he is fighting an almost impossible battle.

An American Tragedy is Dreiser's most important work, for it incorporates all the themes underlying his other novels. The theme is more ambitious: Dreiser does not concentrate on religion, or the artist, or the family, or the businessman. The story of young Clyde Griffiths becomes the story of all America; and beneath the story remains a steady, concentrated focus on a society which tantalizes but never produces.

These basic themes hold the books together. Since a novel needs more than a thematic unity to be successful, however, I shall attempt to evaluate each work as a work of art, showing how Dreiser does or does not do justice to his important stories. My method of analysis is thus thematic and critical, though there are, of course, themes in Dreiser's work other than those I discuss and critical judgments to be made other than those I propose. My hope is to enlarge our understanding of the way in which Dreiser saw his (and our) America by showing how, in his novels, he expressed what he saw. I hope that this study may contribute to our knowing more about the achievement of a particular American writer who confronted peculiarly American themes.

This work owes much to many people who have been of direct or indirect help, but I am especially in debt to Dr. Terence Martin of Indiana University. I would also like to thank the Graduate School of Indiana University (for a grant which enabled me to study the valuable source materials in the Dreiser Collection at the University of Pennsylvania), the Corporation of Yaddo, and Mrs. Myrtle M. Turner who kindly typed the final typescript.

The first chapter is revised from an essay in *Twelve Original Essays on Great American Novels* (Wayne State University Press, 1958, paperback edition 1959), and a brief portion of chapter five appeared in *The New Republic*. The World Publishing Company, Doubleday and Company, and the trustees of the Dreiser estate have generously permitted extensive quotation from a number of Dreiser's works.

CHARLES SHAPIRO

New York City
June 1, 1962

Theodore Dreiser

OUR BITTER PATRIOT

1 SISTER CARRIE AND JENNIE GERHARDT
THE INDIVIDUAL, THE AMERICAN FAMILY, AND THE AMERICAN DREAM

> Life is to be learned as much from books and art as from life itself—almost more so, in my judgment. Art is the stored honey of the human soul, gathered on the wings of misery and travail. Shall the dull and self-seeking and the self-advertising close this store on the groping human mind?
>
> THEODORE DREISER
> "Life, Art and America"

THERE IS A CARELESS GENERALIZATION, perpetuated and intensified by scholarly magazines as well as critical journals, that makes Theodore Dreiser simply a great shaggy monkey pounding the keys of a typewriter who would stumble upon his words—wild words, unbeautiful, unkempt words which, by a transcendental trick left over from the Romantic Period, would pile upon each other and somehow total a powerful novel. A disorganized, crudely written novel, but one with strength and insight. To our regret, however, we are not living in an age of many miracles, and bad sentences, stretched end to end, will never equal a good book.

Dreiser realized this, and while he was an uneven writer, he was conscious of his craftsmanship, and as a result his stories and novels were carefully planned and carefully written. Above all, they were part of his life-long inquiry—his continual grabbing at what he considered to be the vital problems inherent in American life.

Dreiser's novels have an important aim, significant because he was a keen, if often naïve observer of the social and political realities of his day. He saw America as being at middle age, and he was concerned with a culture which, by creating and encouraging artificial goals, was perverting its worthwhile institutions and, more important, was robbing the individual of his chance to live up to a full, meaningful potential. Each of Dreiser's novels illustrates a different aspect of what he felt was a crucial misdirection of American energy. Often his insights were vague and muddied: in *The "Genius"* (1915), for example, Dreiser attempts to explain the forces harmful to the creative artist, and by placing the blame on a curious mixture of capitalism and eroticism his novel rests on a faulty base. Which is to say that Dreiser is usually a bad writer at the point he leaps past his immediate feelings and his own past. In his first two books, *Sister Carrie* (1900) and *Jennie Gerhardt* (1911), Dreiser studies the failure of the American as an individual and of Americans as a family group, and his theme provides a valid and compassionate foundation for the novels. He was writing out of the misery and passion of his own experiences.

Dreiser's works, while exploring many sides to a problem, would adhere to a single point of view, and the focus, often shifting, from book to book, in various economic and philosophical directions, would originate in what he believed at the moment to be the deepest roots of American unhappiness. It is untrue to state, as has been suggested, that Dreiser's art betrays an incapacity for development. His art was never static: only his critics.

Dreiser's technique, while remaining naturalist in spirit, would vary with the American experience explored. The experience which is turned round in *The Bulwark* (1946), (Dreiser's last novel), the disastrous careers of the children of a bed-rock Quaker, is set on a relatively bare stage, while in earlier novels Dreiser's background is a cluttered one, filled with people, facts, musings, and street signs. This profusion of details accentuates the point of view, producing a kaleidoscopic effect. With *The Bulwark* Dreiser settled on a different framework. An almost naked story is told, and the simplicity only adds to the final terror. But this is not true in the first novels, books of tragic courage and predoomed struggle. In these works the well-filled background provides the tone and excuse for the plot.

In *Sister Carrie*, Dreiser's first novel, the details, believed by reviewers to indicate a lack of "style," were ridiculed and parodied, and ever since he has been a sitting duck for critics whose only criterion is a self-oriented meticulousness. Sinclair Lewis, in his Nobel Prize speech, hinted at the shortsightedness of those who would evaluate a new work of art in terms of the standards set up on the basis of other excellent but different efforts.[1] He speculated at the sensation that might have been created if Dreiser had received the award, and Lewis added his own high tribute to a man he saw in the tradition of Whitman and Twain. Only today are we finally understanding that America's rich fictional heritage has a broad enough base to include the shrewd observations of both a Henry James and a Theodore Dreiser. Art, as Edmund Wilson has pointed out, is that which gives meaning to experience, and our experiences and their translation into fiction are many and diverse.

In *Sister Carrie*, the characters, the symbols, the action, and even the details are attuned to a basic theme, an elaboration of Emerson's complaint that "things" dominate the American scene. "Things are in the saddle and ride mankind." [2] Only the "things" had become more elaborate, more slippery to grasp. In later books the burden on the individual would lead to violence and murder. In *Sister Carrie* the rewards are self-destruction, a nagging unhappiness, and a poverty made worse by the visions of former days which promised future glories.

Francis Fergusson defines "action" as that "which points to the object which the dramatist is trying to show us, and we must, in some sense grasp that if we are to understand his complex art; plotting, characterization, versification, thought, and their coherence." [3] In the same sense the themes of Dreiser's novels underlie the books, and unless this is understood, the details and dialogue will give us little more than melodrama. Dreiser's details are carefully injected, seldom robbing his novels of the force of the plots or characterizations which are interesting in themselves. And his details, strategically placed and skillfully ordered, are used to point up his key themes. In *Sister Carrie* the theme is the effect, on the individual consciousness, of the misdirection of the American success dream, and the novel is a logical precursor to *Jennie Gerhardt*.

Details in *Sister Carrie* play up not only the characters but the over-all perception of the novel. Each sordid item is in order, adding illumination to the chapters and adding evidence to the underlying theme —the shame of a society whose structure rested, according to Dreiser, on the shaky premise that guided a man by rewards not in keeping with his potentialities and his promise. And these details are kept from becoming a soapbox squawk against capitalism because Dreiser understands the essential dignity of Hurstwood. Hurstwood, unlike the autonomous figures of "labor" pictured in WPA murals, is detailed into being more than a symbol, and for this reason he is a truer representation of a person and a better symbol.

Dreiser has captured, in the story of Hurstwood and his decline, an almost ideal man and situation to epitomize the essence of early twentieth-century industrial America. Possessing the fatal American yearning for a top role in society, hindered by his strict middle-class concepts, he is forced into various jobs which, by their eclectic nature, put Hurstwood in focus from several points of observation. The first picture catches him as the restaurateur, and as his social status plunges and he switches jobs, we see him increasingly handicapped by his preconceptions of his social position. Hurstwood's downward movement is reemphasized by chance meetings with former acquaintances, so that we are often reminded, as he was, of the point from which he slipped. And we are similarly reminded of the reasons for Hurstwood's fall: chance, material conceit, and his love for Carrie, the three elements which can be symbolically transferred as properties of America. These elements in their larger context would be: problematic changes of fortune, the worship of false values, and the inevitable seduction of the imaginative consciousness by values opposed to a gross materialism, values which might not, in themselves, hold true.

The portrayal of Hurstwood shows how Dreiser uses massive detail to reinforce his theme. We have, for example, a lengthy descriptive passage which introduces Hurstwood, one of the three central figures in the novel, a man whose gradual decline is the paramount human correlative identified with the action of *Sister Carrie*.

At Rector's, Drouet had met Mr. G. W. Hurstwood, manager of Fitzgerald and Moy's. He had been pointed out a very successful and well-known man about town. Hurstwood looked the part, for besides being slightly under forty, he had a good, stout constitution, an active manner, and a solid, substantial air, which was composed in part of his fine clothes, his clean linen, his jewels, and, above all, his own sense of his importance. Drouet immediately conceived a notion of him as being some one worth knowing, and was glad not only to meet him, but to visit the Adams Street bar thereafter whenever he wanted a drink or a cigar.

Hurstwood was an interesting character after his kind. He was shrewd and clever in many little things, and capable of creating a good impression. His managerial position was fairly important—a kind of stewardship which was imposing, but lacked financial control. He had risen by perseverance and industry, through long years of service, from the position of barkeeper in a commonplace saloon to his present altitude. He had a little office where he kept, in a roll-top desk, the rather simple accounts of the place—supplies ordered and needed. The chief executive and financial functions developed upon the owners—Messrs. Fitzgerald and Moy—and upon a cashier who looked after the money taken in.

For the most part he lounged about, dressed in excellent tailored suits of imported goods, a solitaire ring, a fine blue diamond in his tie, a striking vest of some new pattern, and a watch-chain of solid gold, which held a charm of rich design, and a watch of the latest make and engraving. He knew by name, and could greet personally with a "Well, old fellow," hundreds of actors, merchants, politicians, and the general run of successful characters about town, and it was part of his success to do so. He had a finely graduated scale of informality and friendship, which improved from the "How do you do?"

addressed to the fifteen-dollar-a-week clerks and office
attachés, who, by long frequenting of the place, became
aware of his position, to the "Why, old man, how are
you?" which he addressed to those noted or rich individuals who knew him and were inclined to be friendly.
There was a class, however, too rich, too famous, or too
successful, with whom he could not attempt any familiarities of address, and with these he was professionally
tactful, assuming a grave and dignified attitude, paying
them the deference which could win their good feeling
without in the least compromising his own bearing and
opinions. There were, in the last place, a few good fol-
lowers, neither rich nor poor, famous, nor yet remarkably successful, with whom he was friendly on the score
of good-fellow-ship. These were the kind of men with
whom he would converse longest and most seriously. He
loved to go out and have a good time once in a while—
to go to the races, the theatres, the sporting entertainments at some of the clubs. He kept a horse and neat
trap, had his wife and two children, who were well established in a neat house on the North side near Lin-
coln Park, and was altogether a very acceptable individual of our great American upper class—the first grade
below the luxuriously rich.[4]

There are many details in this passage, but they are
in focus and all aim towards the theme. In the first
paragraph we have Hurstwood established as he is seen
by Drouet, a hero admired by an ambitious man.
Hurstwood is then shown as a cautious success, a
moderately rich man typical of Chicago's (and
America's) progress in 1890. We are given a splendid
picture of deceptive ripeness; but the final item in the
initial series, "his own sense of his importance,"
shrewdly questions the meaning of his clothes, linens,
and jewels. We are then told that "he was an interesting character after his own kind," perhaps not a stereotype, but similar enough to his group to lose originality

and to be, like this group, "shrewd and clever in many little things, and capable of creating a good impression." A good impression, of course, in the image of his peers. Hurstwood's job is next introduced, a fitting position for what Hurstwood symbolizes; later, in the novel, his varied occupations will keep pace with the tragic rhythm of his decline. But when we meet him he is a manager of a good restaurant, a man who makes a good front but who lacks financial control and whose position is strictly limited in power. His success, thus under the control of others, can be easily destroyed.

The next paragraph follows up the description, showing the action in terms of his position. He knows his exact role, dresses precisely to it and even modifies his greetings to fit the social position of each customer. This pattern dominates his personal life as well: his home, wife, and all fitting into this "first grade below the luxuriously rich." Not one of the principal characters in the novel is contented with his respective position, for all are aware of a higher group.

This is a lengthy description which we have been given, yet it serves its purpose well, for when Hurstwood and Drouet begin to become aware of one another (Drouet having been similarly set up for us) it is a clash which we can understand, not only in terms of personality differences, but in terms of their social disparity. We see them as subservient to material forces which shape and guide their destinies. We see Hurstwood and Drouet as they see themselves, as they are seen by others, and as Dreiser believes they really are.

Details play up not only the characters but heighten our overall perception of the novel. During the latter part of *Sister Carrie*, when Hurstwood is firmly established as a failure by his own standards, and at the crucial point where his economic status is as low as his personal breakdown, he goes out on an errand for Carrie.

> Hurstwood bought the flour—which all grocers sold in 3½ pound packages—for thirteen cents and paid fifteen cents for a half-pound of liver and bacon. He left the packages, together with the balance of twenty-two cents, upon the kitchen table, where Carrie had found it. It did not escape her that the change was accurate. There was something sad in realizing that, after all, all that he wanted of her was something to eat. She felt as if hard thoughts were unjust. Maybe he would get something yet. He had no vices. [431]

The petty details are in keeping with the fall of a man who once acknowledges his own limited greatness. Hurstwood is now forced to prove his own honesty to himself. It is not that Dreiser wished to record the price of liver and bacon at the turn of the century, but the mundane, stark detail, "thirteen cents," shows Hurstwood's consciousness of the price and Carrie's realization of the sadness of it all. This pressing interest in the exact price of the groceries, the scrupulousness of the exact change on the table, and the final insight of Carrie's into her lover's breakdown, are all ironically emphasized by her reflection that "he had no vices."

The three chief protagonists, Hurstwood, Drouet, and Carrie, have, of course, their own special areas of movement, within which are their own patterns of success and failure. But Drouet and Carrie are the essential part of the Hurstwood story, echoing and reinforcing the theme of a man's dream and his failure. Running underneath the Hurstwood chronicle is the ironic rise of Carrie, the chief protagonist of the novel. Ironic because, while she achieved success, she is never happy by her own standards. And we are reminded at an early stage of her story that she was, in essence, alone, "a lone figure in a tossing, thoughtless sea." [11]

This irony implied in Carrie's ambivalent success story is contrasted with Hurstwood's decline and is in evidence in the middle of the novel. Carrie is participating in an amateur theatrical group. Hurstwood and Drouet are in the audience—and soon the tension of this romantic triangle will force a conclusion. In a Hamlet-like play within a play, Carrie declaims lines which reflect on her own situation. "It is a sad thing to want for happiness, but it is a terrible thing to see another groping about blindly for it, when it is almost within the grasp." [205] And later, "What is it makes you continually war with your happiness?" [207]

Can Carrie ever be happy, could the Hurstwoods ever be content? Dreiser does not believe in the possibility. Dreiser came to New York at roughly the same time as Carrie, and in his book of descriptive pieces on the city *The Color of a Great City* (1923), we see that the problem of the pointlessness of the struggle, though often showing men at their courageous best, was a constant source of wonder to the young reporter. In one of his sketches, "The Toilers of the Tenements," Dreiser described the pitiful conditions of those who toiled in their slum rooms at piece work, at the mercy of greedy employers and grafting police. A random few achieved success.[5]

If this basic theme of individual failure were not present in *Sister Carrie*, if Carrie could be viewed as successful, the critics who dismiss Dreiser would have good reason. His details would show no purpose, and the story would remain melodrama. But the work has a specific orientation and proves what Dreiser's critics could never comprehend, that accurate representation is not inimical to beauty.

Perhaps Drouet is the greatest tragedy of all, for he

unconsciously assumes all the values of his day without a trace of rebellion. As Carrie's discoverer and as the accidental pivot in Hurstwood's life he is necessary to the plot—as the "drummer" of 1890–1920 he will progress to 1956 where he will come face to face with his failure. As Arthur Miller's salesman lies in his grave, the son comments "He had the wrong dreams. All, all wrong . . . He never knew who he was." [6] Drouet is Willy Loman in a more favorable year.

Drouet's life is as lovingly chronicled as Hurstwood's; his love of cigars and good whiskey, his often crude speech, his dress, all are detailed so that we know the man. He is shown to be as helpless and as ambitious as Carrie, a bluff, and a blunderer.

One of the minor figures in the novel shows us Dreiser's methodology at work. Minnie, the sister with whom Carrie boards when she first comes to the city, is a dull prig. In a chapter titled "The Machine and the Maiden: A Knight of Today," we have a short picture of Minnie and her husband. "Minnie was no companion for her sister—she was too old. Her thoughts were staid and solemnly adapted to a condition. If Hanson had any pleasant thoughts or happy feelings he concealed them. He seemed to do all his mental operations without the aid of physical expression. He was as still as a deserted chamber. Carrie, on the other hand, had the blood of youth and some imagination." [57] Carrie thus meets a phlegmatic opposition to her ambitions, and as she becomes more able to adapt to the world Drouet and finally Hurstwood take the place of Minnie.

The price we pay for the Hurstwood of Fitzgerald and Moy's is the Hurstwood of the street-car strike. And as the novel ends Dreiser pictures Carrie at a window in her rocking chair, and he adds, "shall you dream such happiness as you may never feel." [557]

It is precisely this facet of America that in itself holds a balance—the size of the wish is a measurement of the failure. Or as Dreiser once noted as he watched one of New York City's sandwich men, a member of the army of walking signboards who still patrol the streets as a living contrast to whatever they advertise, "To be the antithesis of what life would prefer to be— what could be more degraded than that." [7]

ii

In *Sister Carrie* the theme is the effect, on the individual consciousness, of the misdirection of the American success dream, and eleven years later Dreiser explored the effects of American materialism on the American family in his second novel, *Jennie Gerhardt*. Though the book ostensibly centers on the almost Pollyana-like misfortunes of seduceable Jennie, the theme that strikes through the work is the disastrous consequences the success psychology has on the American family. Two family groups are presented at opposite social and economic poles, and we see them both as separate entities in their own private worlds and as they are in clash with each other. The novel is probably the most autobiographical of Dreiser's fictional works, and while the Gerhardts are not carbon copies of Dreiser's unhappy family, they do represent, in spirit, the author's impressions of his troubled childhood much in the way that *David Copperfield* or *Little Dorrit* convey Dickens' painful evaluations of his early days. The analogy between the Dreisers and the Gerhardts can be seen by comparing *Jennie Gerhardt* with *Dawn* (1931), the first volume of Dreiser's autobiographical chronicles. In *Dawn* Dreiser speaks of "a particularly nebulous, emotional, unorganized and traditionless character," a tragic group which "had somewhere before my birth taken on the complexion of poverty and failure, or, at least seeming failure." [8]

The other family in *Jennie Gerhardt*, the wealthy, socially prominent Kanes, does not stem, of course, from any personal involvement of Dreiser's, and the picture of this group is often blurred and more often exaggerated, for as F. O. Matthiessen pointed out, there was an element in Dreiser of "the poor boy staring hungrily into the bright windows of the rich." [9] But in spite of some glaring artificialities in descriptions and dialogue, the Kanes are forcefully set up in such a way as to reveal the existence of an underlying fatuous economic motivation which proves the wealthy family to be as bereft as the Gerhardts of the needed essentials of family harmony. Like the Gerhardts they were driven to the position of distorting their lives to fit standards set by the nebulous Joneses and the immediate neighbors, but unlike the Gerhardts the problem had advanced far beyond the stage of worrying about meat and shoes.

Jennie is the prop for the novel; as the chief protagonist she is the moral and financial brace of a flabby, poverty ridden family. We first see her in 1880, a girl of eighteen applying, with her mother, for menial work in a Columbus hotel. They are already stamped. "Poverty was driving them. Together they presented so appealing a picture of honest necessity that even the clerk was affected." [10] The Gerhardt family, a large and uncoordinated affair, is presided over in an economically sloppy but morally strait-jacketed fashion by William Gerhardt, an unemployed glass-blower. Besides Jennie the children include Sebastian ("Bass"), Genevieve, George, Martha, William, and Veronica. Bass, like his counterpart in the Kane family, is never spiritually united with the others. As David Riesman observes in his study of the relatively new trend towards "outer-direction" in America's lonely crowd, the older children, if any, "are the privileged guests in a rather second-rate hotel, a hotel whose harassed but smiling managers they put under constant pressure for renovation." [11] Self-centered, conniving but for the most part honest, the children struggle between an allegiance to the family and the powerful pull of standards set up by the outside world, standards which are at constant odds with hearthside preachings. The compromise reached is to face family disasters with a "Well, I wouldn't worry about it . . . we'll get along somehow" attitude. Only when he is literally freed from the family can Bass join the crowd in pursuit of the goals set forth by his contemporaries, comrades in a common rootlessness and a common daydream.

The other Gerhardt children play minor roles, important only as they reinforce the theme of the disintegration of the family and the rejection of the father. As they occasionally pop into the novel they become a rather hazy galaxy of ingrates who, it is assumed, will breed more families of the same type.

Jennie is all suffering, almost too fudgy in her passivity. Seduced by Senator Brander who dies before their child is born, she works as a servant and eventually becomes the mistress of Lester Kane, the "Bass" of the family as rich as the Gerhardts are poor. After much deliberation, societal pressure forces Kane to marry in his own circle, leaving Jennie, who "was never master of her fate," to live a lonely life devoted to others. Jennie was "the product of the fancy, the feeling, the innate affection of the untutored but poetic mind of her mother combined with the gravity and poise which were characteristic of her father." [1] But as Dreiser later points out, "Caged in the world of the material, however, such a nature is almost invariably an anomaly." [15] Meeting misery and insult with a quiet selflessness, she ends her days, appropriately enough, without a real family of her own.

Dreiser is concerned with the family in America, which like Carrie and Hurstwood, is touched and perverted by artificial lures. Thus the children of Dreiser's two families are unsatisfied with any altruistic family orientation and are caught by similar outside forces which swirl them away from the family. It is a profound change in America that Dreiser is cataloging, for in the break from the family comes confusion. The new generation, the Lester Kanes, the Drouets, and the Gerhardt children seem unresponsive to what Dreiser, in an over-sentimental aside, terms "The few sprigs of green that sometimes invade the barrenness of your materialism." [81] When Dreiser's characters are occasionally forced too close to the green they become ill in a social sense and according to the unwritten laws which guide and control, they are temporarily quarantined.

The Gerhardt family, nominally headed by an all-suffering mother and a religious father, is shown as it gradually falls apart. The parents, while respected, are never a pivotal force. The role of the parent in the American family structure was shrinking, and this change, while important in altering the values of the children, is devastating in its effects on the parents. "We live," Dreiser notes, "in an age in which the impact of material forces is well-nigh irresistible; the spiritual nature is overwhelmed by the shock." [132] And the shock to the Gerhardt family is severe, especially as reflected by the pathetic father, burdened by his material failure, haunted by his spiritual drive. He is caught in a vise between old and new values. By the standards of either the old or the new he would be considered a failure. Papa Gerhardt, hurt, confused, is one of the memorable character studies in modern fiction.

At first it appears as if his misfortune is simply the

result of unemployment due to forces beyond his control or interest. But as the family is forced to disperse we see that Papa Gerhardt's situation is more complex. Alone in a strange city, working and sleeping in a factory, he presents a miserable figure. His stiff religiosity forced him to reject Jennie for an immoral action which was obviously sponsored by her devotion to the family which, by his rules, Gerhardt should have been able to support. For the first time in his life he is forced to question his basic beliefs, the ones which have provided the solace and rationale to his career of want and toil. He receives a letter suggesting that the family reunite in Cleveland and start anew.

> And Gerhardt did take this view of the situation. In answer to his wife's letter he wrote that it was not advisable for him to leave his place, but if Bass saw a way for them, it might be a good thing to go. He was the more ready to acquiesce in the plan for the simple reason that he was half distracted with the worry of supporting the family and of paying the debts already outstanding. Every week he laid by five dollars out of his salary, which he sent in the form of a postal order to Mrs. Gerhardt. Three dollars he paid for board, and fifty cents he kept for spending money, church dues, a little tobacco and occasionally a glass of beer. Every week he put a dollar and a half in a little iron bank against a rainy day. His room was a bare corner in the topmost loft of the doorstep of the mill. To this he would ascend after sitting alone on the doorstep of the mill in this lonely, forsaken neighborhood, until nine o'clock of an evening; and here, amid the odor of machinery wafted up from the floor below, by the light of a single tallow candle, he would conclude his solitary day, reading his German paper, folding his hands and thinking, kneeling by an open window in the shadow of the night to say his prayers, and silently stretching himself

to rest. Long were the days, dreary the prospect. Still he lifted his hands in utmost faith to God, praying that his sins might be forgiven and that he might be vouchsafed a few more years of comfort and of happy family life. [104–5]

Dreiser's father had undergone similar separations from his family, and the poignant collection of details which are presented in the paragraph attest to the powerful impression this seclusion must have had on young Theodore. The severe loneliness of the father becomes, for Dreiser, the very worst aspect of the shattered family situation.

Gerhardt's misery increases. Finally, suffering severe injury to his hands, he must return to the family for help. The reunion is a tearful one, the old mill-worker losing control of himself for the moment. He is puzzled by Jennie, admiring her devotion to her child, fearing her apparent relationship with Lester. "Gerhardt went back to his newspaper reading and brooding. His life seemed a complete failure to him and he was only waiting to get well enough to hunt up another job as watchman. He wanted to get out of this mess of deception and dishonesty." [180] When Jennie offers him the hospitality of her home with Lester, Gerhardt rebels. "My whole life comes to nothing." [187] And over and over, querulous and bored, he ponders the value of his life, its apparent purposelessness, its obvious failure.

Ironically Gerhardt's only happiness comes from Vesta, his illegitimate grandchild, the living symbol of Jennie's sin, a sprightly child akin to little Pearl of *The Scarlet Letter*. One day Vesta and Gerhardt go on one of their walks. It was a beautiful spring day.

> Gerhardt took a keen delight in pointing out the wonders of nature to Vesta, and she was quick to respond. Every new sight and sound interested her.

"Oooh! ooh!" exclaimed Vesta, catching sight of a low, flashing touch of red as a robin lighted upon a twig nearby. Her hand was up, and her eyes were wide open.

"Yes," said Gerhardt, as happy as if he himself had but newly discovered this marvelous creature . . . "It is going to look for a worm now. We will see if we cannot find its nest. I think I saw a nest on one of those trees."

He plodded peacefully on, seeking to rediscover an old abandoned nest that he had observed on a former walk . . . "here it is," he said at last, coming to a small and leafless tree, in which a winter-beaten remnant of a home was still clinging. "Here, come now, see" and he lifted the baby up at arm's length. [189–90]

And Gerhardt sadly concludes, "That was a *wren's* nest. They have all gone now. They will not come any more." He trudges back to the house "as if the end of the world had been reached," acutely aware of being, himself, in an alien home.

Minor insults and major rejections come; one of his daughters marries without notifying him, but Gerhardt stolidly offers no comment. "He had had too many rebuffs." [242] He gives up hoping and sinks into a routine gloom and once more goes off alone to work and live in "a wee small corner in the topmost loft of a warehouse." [244] His religious views become increasingly bothersome, and he is finally forced to balance Jennie's sinful goodness against the cold correctness of his other children. "And he was getting so old. He shook his head. Mystery of mysteries. Life was truly strange, and dark, and uncertain. Still he did not want to go and live with any of his children. Actually they were not worthy of him—none but Jennie and she was not good. So he grieved." [245]

During his last years Papa Gerhardt finds a permanent home with Jennie, Lester, and their child. Toler ated by Lester ("The old gentleman oughtn't be so fussy." [254]) he complains about household problems, worrying about small expenses and petty details. "While not very interesting, Gerhardt was not objectionable to Lester, and if the old man wanted to do odd jobs around the big place, why not?" [255] The day of the patriarchal grandfather at the head of the table was gone, the older folk in the American family had already begun to become obsolete, and in a few years Sunday newspaper supplements and countless Ph.D. theses would be devoted to the "problem" of the aged in our midst.

When Gerhardt is dying, Jennie communicates with her brothers and sisters who, characteristically enough, are kept away by other interests. Only Jennie, always kept at a distance by her father as punishment for her great mistake, remains to nurse and comfort him. Finally Gerhardt understands. "You're a good girl . . . You've been to me . . . You forgive me, don't you . . . I understand a lot of things I didn't. We get wiser as we get older." [345] What Gerhardt was unable to fully comprehend was that beneath his financial and moral problems hid the primary cause of his failure: the American materialism had passed the pioneer stage, had distorted values, had made a mockery of family life, and had pre-doomed Gerhardt's honest dream of a happy, secure existence. Dreiser's "comprehensive vision" saw that the evils which brought tragedy to Hurstwood in *Sister Carrie* were inherently antithetical to the continuation of the halcyon days of the American family—if, in truth, the vision of the ideal family organization was ever anything more than a pleasant mirage which was sighted, at a distance, in everyone else's log cabin, in everyone else's Cape Cod cottage.

The universal double standard of preaching morality

and practicing materialism could openly wreck an im-
poverished family, but Dreiser wanted to show that
the effects extended beyond the shacks and slums of
America and entered the homes of the rich. Lester
Kane pities Jennie. "What a family she must have!
What queer non-moral natures they must have to
have brooked such a combination of affairs." [212]
He is oblivious to the parallels with his own family
which, in its fashion, is similarly possessed by another
form of this "queer non-moral nature."

The Kane family, resting firmly and smugly on the
wealth and prestige of a successful first generation
business venture, is constantly guided in its private
affairs by the paramount concern for the good of the
factory. The family is, in fact, a small corporation,
guided by the elder Kane in the role of director. There
is much surface adherence to an understood mutual
admiration, but as in the Gerhardt family, the family
never commands more than a halfhearted respect.
Lester, returning from a business trip, "knew that his
father was around somewhere, but did not bother to
look him up." [148] Kane senior preferred his younger
son Lester, but he displays an overt favoritism for
another son and daughter who successfully fall into
the business pattern. Kane even finds it necessary to
alter his will to bring Lester in line. He understands
that though Lester is temporarily out of his sphere of
control he must eventually return. When he does he
can once again assume his place in the family dynasty
providing he remembers the rules. Just as Papa Gerhardt tries to hold his family together with a misplaced
religious fanaticism, Kane tries holding his family with
a misplaced reliance on position. Neither Gerhardt
nor Kane came close to succeeding, and so the failure
is not only theirs but of the American family and the
American dream.

The failure of the two families to function as cohesive, loving units is the important theme of the novel. However there is still the concern for the individuals who, like Hurstwood, attempt to stage one man rebellions. These mavericks are usually torn from their proper positions by the lure of a woman, and in the case of Senator Brander it is Jennie who provides the attraction. Brander is not a fully developed character, a rather sketchy caricature of a middle-aged statesman. "In him there were joined, to a remarkable degree the wisdom of the opportunist and the sympathetic nature of the true representative of the people." [19] It is the second element in his makeup which brought him close to Jennie.

Lester has the same two qualities. Well aware of his constant life of sham, he still spouts platitudes of the day in an unending stream. "Hew to the line, let the chips fall where they may" was his pet motto, "Keep young or die young" was another, and he admonishes his mistress to "look facts in the face." [198, 270, 217] All pleasant enough bromides by themselves, all revealing sayings when repeated and believed. Dreiser sums up Lester as being blessed with a fine imagination and considerable insight but as lacking "the ruthless, narrow-minded insistence on his individual superiority which is a necessary element in almost every great business success." [303] He is an unsuccessful imitation of Senator Brander, compounded of the same two elements in differing proportions, and for this reason he is less able to cope with his break from the established pattern of behavior. Lester was, above all, "an essentially animal-man, pleasantly veneered by education and environment." [133] His death was from a lesion of a major blood-vessel in his brain and not from the anticipated intestinal trouble; it was not his wealth but the problems it forced that stifled his life. It was not the desire for Jennie but the problems this desire brought forth that smashed his ambition.

The two rebels, Brander and Kane, are both brought back to camp, one by death and one by resignation, and the two families are shown to be ineffective. But there has been a struggle, and in this struggle lies both the wonder and truth of the humanity which Dreiser portrays.

But at what point does the struggle come? For both Hurstwood and Kane it came in middle life. "There comes a time in every thinking man's life when he pauses and 'takes stock' of his condition; when he asks himself how it fares with his individuality as a whole, mental, moral, physical, material. This time comes after the first heedless flights of youth have passed, when the initiative and more powerful efforts have been made, and he begins to feel the uncertainty of results and final values which attaches itself to everything." [192]

Dreiser also saw America as being at middle-age. As Professor Vivas and others have pointed out, he was not an orderly philosopher with a defined system. His announced conversion to Marxism (Communist Party, U. S. A. version) in his last years was a token gesture and not, as he claimed, the logical culmination of his life, or at least not of his life as revealed in his literary works. All that Dreiser does in *Jennie Gerhardt* is caution us to look around, to see, as in *Sister Carrie*, what has happened to the individual in America, and specifically, to understand what was happening to the American family. Whether or not Dreiser's insights were accurate for his time is debatable . . . there can be little quarrel about their present application.

THE FINANCIER, THE TITAN, THE STOIC
THE AMERICAN GIANT

> In America, the history of our financiers is so full of thievery and selfishness as to appear comic were it not for the mass misery which so many of their deeds involved. . . . For the individual and the mass are interdependent facts, and the one cannot escape the other, try as each may. . . . One thing is sure: the individual cannot wholly understand the mass, nor the mass the individual. Both have their significance, their place, but if one were to say of either that it or he alone had claim to significance as a helpful factor in life, or as dramatic or artistic material, or as a spectacle, one would be greatly mistaken. Both have. All have.
>
> THEODORE DREISER
> "The American Financier"

"THE FINANCIER" presented a new approach to the American dream. For now Dreiser was not dealing with failures but with a man who had the capacity and guile to become a living representative of the successful capitalist, replete with all the assorted trimmings—culture, fame, and most important of all, women. Dealing with a successful protagonist, however, created new problems for Dreiser, and the critic concerned with the Cowperwood trilogy (*The Financier* [1912], *The Titan* [1914], and *The Stoic* [1947]) must face new critical questions.

Dreiser's businessman hero, Frank Cowperwood, was based, in most essentials, on the checkered but steadily sensational career of Charles Tyson Yerkes, and, if nothing else, the three novels present us with a staggering amount of documented material on the intricate machinations involved in capturing and controlling the traction lines of American and English cities. Dreiser was a tireless researcher.[1] One noted scholar has remarked that the Cowperwood volumes "contain perhaps the greatest mass of documentation to be found in any American novels in the naturalistic tradition. They are records of an epoch of American life." [2] But unlimited documentation has its drawbacks, and Dreiser had to strive to make his material meaningful, to give us not merely case histories but novels.

The chief problem was inherent in the character of Yerkes-Cowperwood himself. Jennie Gerhardt, Carrie Meeber, Hurstwood, and Papa Gerhardt were all victims, and though we are perhaps skeptical of their ambitions we surely pity their almost inevitable failures. Dreiser, in a sense, loaded the dice in his first two novels.

Carrie and Jennie were not the only focal points for the novels in which they appear, but only part of larger dramas. Cowperwood, on the other hand, by the very nature of his strength, his success, his vigor, dominates *The Financier* and the other novels in which he appears, for he *is* the financier. All characters exist as part of his story. They are reflectors, in the Jamesian sense, of his triumphs and conquests. We can see their stories only in terms of Cowperwood, as they help or hinder the maverick businessman. Their weakness is contrasted to his ambition, their lives hinge on his. In *The Stoic* one of the minor characters "must proceed to disturb all his present arrangement in order to accommodate and make possible and pleasant this other man's brisk and dauntless progress through life!" [3] This is a one man novel, in structure and in story, and Dreiser never seems to fully master this new concept. It is almost a Dreiserian paradox—the stronger the hero, the weaker the novel. Cowperwood meets with failures in *The Financier*, he is feeling his way in the world of finance, and the novel is powerful. But *The Titan* and *The Stoic*, chronicling his fantastic successes, are wearisome and inept, worthy precursors of *Cash McCall* and other modern novels of high finance —books with nothing but "happy problems" [4] confronting entrepreneurs with all the humanity to be found in the grotesque balloon giants that feature Thanksgiving Day parades.

ii

Cowperwood has been called an immoral creation and *The Financier* has been attacked as an immoral book. A typical comment is found in an essay by Stuart P. Sherman which first appeared in 1915.[5] He notes that Dreiser's "jungle-motive results in a dreary monotony" and that "He has just two things to tell us about Cowperwood; that he has a rapacious appetite for money, and that he has a rapacious appetite for women. . . . he 'documents' these two truths about Cowperwood in seventy-four chapters, in each of which he shows us how this hero made money or how he captivated women in Philadelphia."

And the character of Cowperwood has been praised. "He [Dreiser] raised Cowperwood-Yerkes to the level of destiny, where another might have debased him below the level of society. Cowperwood becomes another Tamerlane; and as one remembers not the cities that Tamerlane sacked, but the character that drove him to conquest and the Oriental world that made that character possible, so one sees Cowperwood as the highest expression of the acquisitive society in which he rules so commandingly." Alfred Kazin adds that Cowperwood must accept less from life "because he has surged beyond its traditional limitations." [6]

Cowperwood is no carbon copy of Yerkes, but as F. O. Matthiessen states, "Dreiser's amplest expression of what he understood of the time-spirit, his contribution to the myth of the American hero." [7] Dreiser carefully establishes the background of his hero, this man of whom "There was no more escaping the greatness that was inherent in him than there was for so many others the littleness that was in them." [8] Cowperwood is as big as others are small, and Cowperwood is hard, developing at the start of his career a philosophy devoid of illusions.

> Frank Algernon Cowperwood was not a weakling given to wild ideas of financial prosperity; he was not of the kind who in prosperity cuts throats and in disaster sits down and weeps over their own woes. Whatever he was he was neither a hypocrite nor a fool. He did not capitalize the future. . . . He based everything on thought, after he made due allowance for chance and opportunity, which he could not control. He was no fatalist. . . . He was no coward; and above all, he was no moralist. . . . People talked and talked. . . . only as a rule they were not quick and clever as he was. For this, sometimes, he was sorry for them. At other times he was not. He knew he had a splendid mind. He knew he had a marvelous physique. He knew he had a magnetic and dominating will. Few people, in extremes, could face him out. . . . he could almost, in the face of defeat, snatch success from the hands of fate. He had done it time and again. [432]

Cowperwood has more than calculated ambition. He is perceptive, and even at the apprentice stage is a wizard at understanding how to benefit from the seemingly complicated world of stocks and bonds. As a child he bought goods from a wholesale auctioneer and peddled the stock, at a considerable profit, to an admiring Philadelphia grocer. Later in life he was to comment that "his brain was his office." [50]

Dreiser makes a point of stressing that Cowperwood's strength derives, in part, from his attitude towards the weak. "There were the weak and the strong." [40] Unburdened with conscientious scruples, he always considered himself financially honest. [192] "First you secured the money. Then you secured the reputation. The two things were like two legs on which you walked. Then your mere word was as good as money, or better." [125]

"Weakness" according to Cowperwood, was "the real crime in an individual." [414] Certainly he was an opportunist. [264] He wanted money, not for its sake alone, but for what it would control, "for what it will represent in the way of dignity, force, power." [350] And how to amass this control? By force, "great mental and physical force. Why, these giants of commerce and money could do as they pleased in this life." [243]

His attitudes on social issues were predictable. "He was not disturbed by the cause of slavery, or the talk of the secession, or the general progress or decline of the country, except in so far as it affected his immediate interests." [91] Cowperwood considered the Negroes as inherently inferior, and "he saw no particular reason why the south should not protest vigorously against the destruction of their property and their system." [155] Early in his career he remarks that the Negro "isn't worth all this excitement. . . . It's hurting our Southern trade." [63]

Ruthless and successful, Cowperwood has been

called by one critic "a figure of wish-fulfillment, in whom the author has embodied and realized all the desires to which circumstances have denied satisfaction in his own life." [9] Cowperwood, Whipple continues, is a "resplendent demigod." But how did the demigod evolve. Dreiser carefully details the childhood: the passive father, one of the "incomparable old men" [10] Dreiser created so well; the successful uncle; young Frank's defeating the neighborhood bully; and the famous lesson of the lobster and the squid, on display at a nearby fish-market.

> The lobster and the squid came well along in his fish experiences; he was witness of a familiar tragedy in connection with these two, which stayed with him all his life and cleared things up considerably intellectually. The squid, it appeared from the talk of the idle bystanders who were always loafing about this market, was considered the rightful prey of the lobster; and the latter had no other food offered him. The lobster lay at the bottom of the clear glass tank on the yellow sand, apparently seeing nothing—you could not tell in which way his beady, black buttons of eyes were looking—but apparently they were never off the body of the squid. The latter, pale and waxy in texture, looking very much like pork fat or jade, was moving about in torpedo fashion; but his movements were apparently never out of the eyes of his enemy, for by degrees small portions of his body began to disappear, snapped off by the relentless claws of his pursuer. The latter, as young Cowperwood was one day a witness, would leap like a catapult to where the squid was apparently idly dreaming, and the squid, very alert, would dart away, shooting out at the same time a cloud of ink, behind which it would disappear. It was not always completely successful, however. Some small portions of its body or its tail were frequently left in the claws of the monster below. Days passed, and, now fascinated by the drama, young Cowperwood came daily. [11]

Frank keeps coming back to observe the tank, for he liked "to study the rough claw with which the lobster did his deadly work. He liked to stare at the squid and think how fateful was his doom." [13] Unfortunately, he misses the final kill, and he stares at the slain squid, then at the killer:

"That's the way it has to be, I guess," he commented to himself. "That squid wasn't quick enough. He didn't have anything to feed on." He figured it out. The squid couldn't kill the lobster—he had no weapon. The lobster could kill the squid—he was heavily armed. There was nothing for the squid to feed on; the lobster had the squid as prey. What was the result to be? What else could it be? "He didn't have a chance," he said, finally, tucking his books under his arm and trotting on.

It made a great impression on him. It answered in a rough way that riddle which had been annoying him so much in the past: "How is life organized?" Things lived on each other—that was it. . . . He wasn't so sure about men living on men yet. [13–14]

"For days and weeks Frank thought of this and of the life he was tossed into, for he was already thinking of what he should be in this world, and how he should get along. From seeing his father count money, he was sure that he would like banking; and Third Street, where his father's office was, seemed to him the cleanest, brightest, most fascinating street in the world." [14–15]

Throughout *The Financier* we are reminded, directly or indirectly, of the lobster-squid drama. During his early career as a Philadelphia stock broker Cowperwood was a fascinated, open-mouthed admirer of the excitable manipulations of his elders. But he observed carefully.

Buying and selling stocks, as he soon learned, was an art, a subtlety, almost a psychic emotion. Suspicion, intention, feeling—these were the things to be "long" on. You had to know what a certain man was thinking of— why, you could not say—and suspect that he was going to buy or unload a given amount—why, you could not say. If you had a big buying or a big selling order, it was vitally important that your emotions, feeling, or subtlest thought should, by no trick of thought transference, telepathy, facial expression, or unguarded mood on your part be conveyed to any other person. [83]

The lobster, too, apparently saw nothing.

"To get what you could and hold it fast." [103] This became Cowperwood's creed. On the stock exchange he was a junior dynamo, "snapping bargains right from under the teeth of his rivals," [106] yet keeping a pose of respectable condescension. And as he proceeded on his career, he cornered and exploited the Philadelphia transit system, finally being sent to jail for his financial crimes but never losing his shrewdness, never forgetting his early observations at the fish market. "Wealth, the position, and force which means give, was to him as his right arm. He could . . . like the lobster, grow another claw." [378–79]

Dreiser constantly uses animal comparisons, emphasizing the jungle atmosphere of big business, and more especially of little business trying to be big. One political and business failure had his carcass "as rapidly and as effectively picked clean and bare to the bones as this particular flock of political buzzards knew how to pick him." [470] And he makes the observation "Such is life." When Cowperwood discards his first wife and two children he thinks of fish dying on a shore, having no value "save to those sea-feeding buzzards which sit on the shores of some coasts and wait for such food." [483] And once more "It is a pitiable spectacle—a gruesome one; but it is life."

A few more examples. "They were all hawks—he and they. They were all tigers facing each other in a financial jungle . . . wolves at one moment, smiling, friendly human beings at another. Such was life. He had no illusions." [354] Stock brokers are like a lot of gulls, "hanging on the lee of the wind, hungry and anxious to snap up any unwary fish." [84] And in prison Cowperwood reflects that one forceful man respects another. "They are like wolves and tigers that run best in packs. They may eat one another ultimately, but never so long as there is anything else to eat." [704]

After leaving prison, Cowperwood regains his fortune and, with his mistress Aileen (later to become his wife, and just as predictably, to be thrown over for a series of other women) decides to conquer Chicago. *The Financier* ends with the culmination of Cowperwood's Philadelphia days. And, predictably, he leaves Philadelphia with a fortune gained, during a stock market crash, gained at the expense of others less cunning, less opportunistic. "Like a wolf prowling under glittering, bitter stars in the night, he was looking down into the humble folds of simple men and seeing what their ignorance and their unsophistication would cost them." [770] In a few days he remakes a million dollars, and now his future lay clear and straight before him. A future, of course, determined by his past—by a past and a philosophy which reaches back to the memorable day when the lobster finally destroyed his weak opponent.

While Dreiser's use of animal imagery is surprisingly successful, *The Financier*, the first and only important novel of the trilogy, does have its lamentable spots of awkward, insipid, and almost clichéd writing. Dreiser refers to the "hymneal yoke," [115] and a neighborhood bully is described as a "pyrotechnic rowdy." [5] Oddly enough (but not so odd if we bear in mind the revelations of his childhood found in his autobiographical writings), Dreiser seems obviously ill at ease when dealing with the shadier members of society: crooked politicians, Pinkerton men, and prostitutes. "In a few moments the 'madam," as the current word characterized this type of woman, appeared." [510–11]

Dreiser overuses and misuses words such as "trig" and "eventuate." In describing Cowperwood's appearance he tells us that "Nature had destined him to be about five feet ten inches tall." [47] And in a recital of the youthful financier's many romantic adventures, the bold, naturalistic author mentions Marjorie Stafford, but teases us off with "Shall the story of Marjorie be told? It isn't as innocent as the others. But, no, let it go. There will be more than sufficient without it." [39]

Dreiser, like many other novelists, is at his worst when preaching, when he casts aside his role of narrator to comment and philosophize. His bonus asides to the reader are often monumental bores. At an early part of Cowperwood's meteoric career we are told about "life" and "love." "Life," Dreiser announces, "takes on a peculiar and curious light when love enters. Ordinarily it is sickled o'er by the pale cast of reflection, wearisome and drab; but when love enters, it is as though the sun rose after a dreary stretch of weather —the world becomes roseate once more." [95]

And the conclusion of *The Financier* is almost a parody of itself. It is a mawkish section entitled "The Magic Crystal" which follows a discussion of a fish (the Black Grouper) which is to the fish world what Cowperwood is to his business universe. Here is the final paragraph of the novel, an excellent microcosm of Dreiser's chief defects.

The three witches that hailed MacBeth upon the
blasted heath might in turn have called to Cowperwood, "Hail to thee, Frank Cowperwood, master of a
great railway system! Hail to thee, Frank Cowperwood,
Builder of a priceless mansion! Hail to thee, Frank Cowperwood, patron of arts and possessor of endless riches!
Thou shalt be famed hereafter." But like the Weird Sisters, they would have lied, for in the glory was also the
ashes of Dead Sea fruit—an understanding that could
neither be inflamed by desire nor satisfied by luxury; a
heart that was long since wearied by experience; a soul
that was as bereft of illusion as a windless moon. And to
Aileen, as to Macduff, they might have spoken a more
pathetic promise, one that concerned hope and failure.
To have and not to have! All the seeming, and yet the
sorrow of not having! Brilliant society that shone in a
mirage, yet locked its doors; love that eluded as a will-o'-
the-wisp and died in the dark. "Hail to thee, Frank
Cowperwood, master and no master, prince of a world of
dreams whose reality was sorrow!" So might the
witches have called, the bowls have danced with figures,
the fumes with vision, and it would have been true.
What wise man might not read from such a beginning,
such an end? [780]

This is bad, exaggerated writing, as phony and senti-
mental as can be. But, even admitting such miserable
moments, *The Financier* moves us, for much of the
writing is clear and forceful, and the character of
Cowperwood never gets out of hand as it does in the
following volumes of the trilogy.

Dreiser does attempt to understand his hero. "It
would be too much to say that Cowperwood's mind
was of the first order. It was subtle enough in all conscience—and involved, as is common with the executive great, with a strong sense of personal advancement. It was a big mind . . . but he could not
be sure . . . whatever . . . was important for

him." [700] And Dreiser attempts to understand the
people around Cowperwood. As a result much of *The
Financier* manages to reach us and move us as most
business novels do not. Ludwig Lewisohn has referred
to the pity of Dreiser's "large heart out of which he had
created his incomparable old men." [11] There are at least
three of these memorable characters present in *The
Financier*: Cowperwood's father, Henry; the Irish
political boss, Butler; and the ineffective Stener. Each,
of course, weaker than Frank Cowperwood, each hurt,
in different ways, by Cowperwood's boom and bust
career in Philadelphia.

Old Cowperwood, by nature doomed to middle-
class mediocrity, is filled with the platitudes of a
Babbitt, but lacks the vision and drive to see beyond
them. "He looked upon life as a business situation or
deal, with everybody born as more or less capable
machines to take a part in it. It was surprising to him
to see how many incapable or unsatisfactory machines
there were; but, thank Heaven, now that he was getting along fairly well this was no affair of his." [2]

This is Henry Cowperwood as we first met him, a
man lacking "magnetism." Succeeding at his bank, he
reacts predictably. He moves his family to a better
neighborhood and buys Chippendale furniture, now
"the rage of the day." [64] He entertains a number
of people "who were about as successful as himself,
heads of small businesses who traded at his bank—
dealers in dry-goods, leather, groceries (wholesale),
and grain." His children have classier friends, and his
wife begins to hold afternoon teas.

As he rises with his son, so he must fall with him. As
Frank loses prestige and money and goes to jail, all as
an indirect result of a financial panic caused by the
great Chicago fire, Old Cowperwood becomes a
wrecked man, as miserable in his way as Papa Ger-

hardt, and equally unsure of what caused his calamity. Henry Cowperwood, an elderly, broken gentleman, is forced to retire from a high position in his bank and resume work as a clerk:

> To see old Cowperwood bustling off from his new but very much reduced home at half after seven in the morning in order to reach the small bank, which was some distance away and not accessible by street-car line, was one of those pathetic sights which the fortunes of trade so frequently offer. He carried his lunch in a small box because it was inconvenient to return home in the time alloted for this purpose, and because his new salary did not permit the extravagance of a purchased one. It was his one ambition now to eke out a respectable but unseen existence until he should die, which he hoped would not be long. Day in and day out he went shuttlewise back and forth in this manner, pointed out occasionally by those who had known him in his better days as the ex-president of the Third National who had come to grief through his son. He was a pathetic figure with his thin legs and body, his gray hair, and his snow-white side-whiskers. He was very lean and angular, and, when confronted by a difficult problem, a little uncertain or vague in his mind. The habit of putting his hand to his mouth and of opening his eyes in an assumption of surprise, which had no basis in fact, grew upon him. He really degenerated into a mere automaton. [732–33]

Edward Malia Butler could adjust, with much greater ease, to the swift pace of the Philadelphia business world. A successful Irish immigrant who began by gathering slop for pigs and managed to charm and bully his way up in politics, he befriends the ambitious Frank Cowperwood. When Frank, already married, has an affair with his daughter, Aileen, Butler is strong enough to act, though Cowperwood does eventually take his daughter away.

Like most men of affairs, Cowperwood included, he was mistrustful of people in general, looking on them as aimless forces rather than as self-regulating bodies, though he was nevertheless religious-minded. Nothing save the will of God could save anybody in the long run; but you were in duty bound to help God by helping yourself. Such was his philosophy. The devil represented all untoward forces within and without ourselves which made people—weak elements—do the strange things they did. He could not have explained life any better than that; but in a rough way he felt that he was serving God when he did his best to punish Cowperwood and save Aileen. [498]

The home life of Butler, his red-faced, home-loving wife, and their four ambitious children is described with affection and wit. The faithful, clumsy Mrs. Butler is constantly mystified by the social rise of her husband and by the fierce and often unfeeling complaints of her sons and daughters, children who are somewhat ashamed of their parents' rough manners. A typical family meal is given us, and here, as in many other scenes, Dreiser's details, often criticized as being formless masses of information, do give us a picture of just what the Butlers were like, in what ways they suffer, in what ways they are good people. The scene begins with Aileen making a familiar complaint. "Papa, why do we stay in this old barn?" The father affectionately protests. "I don't see anything the matter with this house. Your mother and I manage to live in it well enough." [202–3] The fight begins. Reference is made to the fact that the Frank Cowperwoods have built a new stylish house. Mrs. Butler now moves as a peacemaker, a role she has undoubtedly played many times before.

"Children! Children!" (Mr. Butler, for all his commercial and political responsibility, was as much a child to her as any.) "Youse mustn't quarrel now. Come now. Give your father the tomatoes."

There was an Irish maid serving at the table; but plates were passed from one to another just the same. A heavily ornamented chandelier, holding sixteen imitation candles in white porcelain, hung low over the table and was brightly lighted, another offense to Aileen.

"Mama, how often have I told you not to say 'youse'?" pleaded Norah, very much disheartened by her mother's grammatical errors. "You know you said you wouldn't."

"And who's to tell your mother what she should say?" called Butler, more incensed than ever at this sudden and unwarranted rebellion and assault. "Your mother talked before ever you was born, I'd have you know. If it weren't for her workin' and slavin' you wouldn't have any fine manners to be paradin' before her. I'd have you know that. She's a better woman nor any you'll be runnin' with this day, you little baggage, you!"

"Mama, do you hear what he's calling me?" complained Norah, hugging close to her mother's arm and pretending fear and dissatisfaction.

"Eddie! Eddie!" cautioned Mrs. Butler, pleading with her husband. "You know he doesn't mean that, Norah. Don't you know he doesn't?"

She was stroking her baby's head. The reference to her grammar had not touched her at all.

Butler was sorry that he had called his youngest a baggage; but these children—God bless his soul—were a great annoyance. Why, in the name of all the saints, wasn't this house good enough for them? [204]

At this point the older boys calm the troubled waters, for "both realized that the house was old and poorly arranged; but Mr. and Mrs. Butler liked it, and business sense and family peace dictated silence on this score." [203] Again Dreiser shows he understands how to catch the essence of the American family, and the writing is sufficiently polished to placate even the over-tender sensibilities of the most fastidious new critic.

Cowperwood's courage and audacity is in obvious, planned contrast to the unfortunate, shoddy cowardice of George W. Stener who, as city treasurer, takes much of the blame for the financier's blatant misuse and juggling of public funds. When the heat is finally put on, Cowperwood knows how to behave and behaves in a cool, practical fashion. Facing jail, he places his personal and business affairs in the best possible shape. "During all this whirl of disaster he never once lost his head or his courage." [476] But Stener, a typical, lack-lustre party hack, collapses and takes to bed. Significantly enough, he had been forewarned but refused to believe and was incapable of acting. "A new suit of brown clothes that ten days before fitted him perfectly now hung on him loosely." [478]

Mrs. Stener is dumbfounded, but as Dreiser observes, "Sometimes the mediocre and the inefficient attain to a classic stature when dignified by pain." [480] She realized that her husband's prosperity was over, that the Chicago fire and his link with Cowperwood had ruined him. "In the agonized expression of his face she read all the horrors of debasement and difficulty with which he invested the future. Their property was to be swept away; their children reduced to penury. Like every dependent woman of this class, usually far more resourceful than her lord and master, she tried to help him think." [479] Finally, one day, she reads the morning paper and notes the item that the Citizen's Municipal Reform Association accuses her husband of pilfering five hundred thousand dollars. She questions him, asking if the sum is correct. "I think so," he admitted weakly, "I'm not quite sure yet. It may be less." [480] All Mrs. Stener can do is stare and twist her hands.

We are, of course, prepared for Stener's muddled behavior. Earlier in *The Financier* one of the political
leaders of Philadelphia contrasts Cowperwood and
Stener. Cowperwood, he properly reasons, is shrewder,
more farseeing and calculating, and "not less dishon-
est." But Stener "was lacking in force and brains—not
morals. This lack was his principal crime." [387] A
crime in a business world where you had to either use
or be used, fight or be destroyed, lobster or squid.

Even in prison Cowperwood succeeds in forcing his
personality over others. Chapin, a minor prison functionary, is highly flattered when Cowperwood recalls
his name and Cowperwood is catered to and made
comfortable. Chapin, a Quaker, is described as a
fatherly, kindly old man "having faith in those shib-
boleths of the weak and inexperienced mentally—
human justice and human decency." [693] Cowperwood senses all this and is ready at once to exploit the
man. Though always out for himself, Cowperwood
does feel pity for those not as resourceful as he always
proves to be. Watching a fellow prisoner, an obvious
predestined failure, Cowperwood feels sorry and considers "the stress of life that had no doubt staggered
and overcome his feeble intellect." And he wonders
"who was to straighten out the matter of the unjust
equipment with which most people began?" How
could they become important, "how save their pointless lives?" [660]

We feel certain that Cowperwood believes he is doing good for the public as well as for himself; and his
plotting does result in better surface transportation;
better, cheaper, and more efficient. Eliseo Vivas rec-
ognizes that Cowperwood "is propelled by a strong
will directed to the conquest of power and reckless of
the claims of society in its search for satisfaction. But
even Cowperwood is not entirely destructive, and his

genius, in the pursuit of its own arbitrary end, has a constructive side." [12]

His business methods are ruthless but practical. His enemies are usually equally corrupt. He is part of a far-reaching pragmatic ethic. As the judge who sentences him comments to Stener, "the mis-application of public money has become the great crime of the age. If not promptly and firmly checked, it will ultimately destroy our institutions." [675] This, of course, was the age when big business press-agented itself into American hearts as a public benefactor. We all plead, at some time, "the necessity of life." [164] The financier, the crooked politician are unfortunate parts of American life, but, as Dreiser points out, we are all sinners. Most of us are not shocked "to the point of protesting." We are, in a sense, responsible for the Cowperwoods. Dreiser is not muckraking in *The Financier* any more than he is whitewashing. He is telling us a story of a powerful man, a strong force who influences weaker men and is, in the end, defeated because of their weakness.

iii

The Titan and *The Stoic* are inferior works, mostly because Cowperwood turns quickly into a flat parody of Yerkes, perhaps because Dreiser bewitched himself with his own image of his hero. "On the other hand, in the nation at large there was growing up a feeling that at the top there were a set of giants— Titans—who, without heart or soul, and without any understanding of or sympathy with the condition of the rank and file, were setting forth to enchain and enslave them." [13]

To Ford Madox Ford *The Titan* was simply a rendering of "normal life a few years ago when life

was simpler and less corrupt." [14] In any case, the out-
look on life is simpler than in the first volume of the
trilogy. Cowperwood almost conquers Chicago, and he
falls in love with a succession of women, finally meeting the big love of his life, Berenice, the young daughter of the proprietress of a fashionable Louisville
brothel. In *The Stoic,* a novel Dreiser labored over
many years, [15] and which finally was published post-
humously, Cowperwood invades London, falls ill and
dies before his plans for an art museum and charity
hospital can be realized. *The Stoic* ends with the
lengthy spiritual conversion of Berenice, who visits
India and finally dedicates her life to the service of
others while freely quoting eastern philosophers.
"What was it that the Guru had said of charity? Be
thankful for the opportunity to give to others. Be
grateful that by helping a poor man, you are able to
help yourself. For, is not the universe yourself? If a
man comes to your door, go and meet yourself." [305]

The Stoic is undoubtedly Dreiser's feeblest effort,
bad because of unrelieved, laborious descriptions of
business dealings, because of hoked up philosophical
digressions that would do shame even to a freshman
philosophy major, and because of generous quantities
of atrocious writing: "her brain was a whirl of emotion," and "he adjusted his monocle the better where-
with to contemplate him." [139, 153] Occasional attempts at humor are heavy-handed.

It is a shame that of Dreiser's three novels (sub-
titled "A Trilogy of Desire"), only the first comes off.
But perhaps "desire" is a difficult concept to catch
hold of, and certainly we should be grateful that
Dreiser carried Cowperwood successfully through the
formative years. *The Financier* tells us much about
Cowperwood, *The Titan* and *The Stoic* gave us alter-
nate doses of financial facts and mystical philosophy.

The Financier is a novel in the true sense, a planned work of art and it is still the best fictional study of the American businessman; *The Titan* and *The Stoic* have a negative virtue in that they help to show us just how splendid *The Financier* really is.

3 THE "GENIUS"
THE AMERICAN ARTIST AND
THE AMERICAN DREAM

> The significance of scenes in general which hold and
> bind our lives for us, making them sweet or grim according
> to the sharpness of our perceptions, is a wonderful thing.
> We are passing among them every moment. A new arrange-
> ment is had with every move we make. If we but lift our
> eyes we see a variation which is forever interesting and for-
> ever new.
>
> THEODORE DREISER
> "The Beauty of Life"

TODAY, when so many paintings look like the disorganized splatterings of flamboyant madmen, so
many poems seem to exist as post-graduate exercises
in verbal camouflage, and so many novels are peripheral to any meaningful experience, a discussion of the
artist and his relationship to American society can
easily degenerate into an exercise in wishful thinking.
But it is an old and honorable theme, a continual and
ever changing dilemma, an unresolved dialectic which
Theodore Dreiser faced in his long, sprawling novel,
The "Genius" (1915), a book dealing with the American artist and his search for a place in American life.

This story has its beginnings in the town of Alexandria,
Illinois, between 1884 and 1889, at the time when the
place had a population of somewhere near ten thou-

sand. There was about it just enough of the air of a city
to relieve it of the sense of rural life. It had one street-
car line, a theatre,—or rather, an opera house, so-called
(why no one might say, for no opera was ever performed
there)—two railroads, with their stations, and a business
district, composed of four brisk sides to a public square.
In the square were the county courthouse and four newspapers. These two morning and two evening papers
made the population fairly aware of the fact that life
was full of issues, local and national, and that there were
many interesting and varied things to do. On the edge of
town, several lakes and a pretty stream—perhaps Alexandria's most pleasant feature—gave it an atmosphere
not unakin to that of a moderate-priced summer resort.
Architecturally the town was not new. It was mostly
built of wood, as all American towns were at this time,
but laid out prettily in some sections, with houses that
sat back in great yards, far from the streets, with flower
beds, brick walks, and green trees as concomitants of a
comfortable home life. Alexandria was a city of young
Americans. Its spirit was young. Life was all before almost everybody. It was really good to be alive.[1]

Thus, smoothly and beautifully, begins Dreiser's
novel about the American artist, his fight for recogni-
tion, his bohemian attitudes, his struggles with the
forces of a conservative American capitalism that try
to lead his talents into conformity. The first section of
The "Genius" entitled "Youth," is possibly Dreiser's
best writing, full of youthful desires and practical hardships in the career of Eugene Witla, who leaves
Alexandria, works in Chicago at odd jobs and finally
discovers himself as a newspaper illustrator. Coming
to New York City, he begins his career as a painter
and magazine illustrator. "Youth" ends with Witla
about to marry Angela Blue, a farm girl who is older
and much more conservative than the eager, inde-
pendent artist. It is obviously a predoomed marriage,

similar in many details to Dreiser's own unhappy experience. Dreiser captures the excitement of Witla's growth, and we sympathize with and glory in the young man's first artistic plunges. Unfortunately, from this point on the book is a dreary failure.

Perhaps, as Robert Spiller suggests, biography is too closely followed, and perhaps this is especially true in the later sections of *The "Genius"* ("Struggle" and "Revolt"). "Witla's career is checkered as Dreiser's had been by a nervous breakdown followed by a long period of business success, during which his art died." [2] Mrs. Dreiser tells us that Eugene Witla is a composite of the lives of three men, "the artist Everett Shinn by whom he was fascinated, and the physical and nervous form of a young art editor of the Buttrick Publications, who had committed suicide, imposed upon the structure of Dreiser himself." [3]

In order to understand what qualities make some of Dreiser's work so powerful, it is interesting to contrast the first and later sections of *The "Genius,"* to study the success of "Youth" and then to try to explain what went wrong in "Struggle" and "Revolt," what made such an excellent critic as F. O. Matthiessen call *The "Genius"* Dreiser's poorest novel.[4]

ii

In *The Stoic* Frank Cowperwood, who is establishing an important art collection, remarks, "I have tried to bring into my life . . . the beauty which is entirely outside of cities and business." [256] Art always had a fascination for the financier, and he "sympathized with the artistic spirit, believed that after wealth and feminine beauty it was the one great thing. Perhaps wealth and beauty and material art forms—the arts and crafts of the world—were indissolubly linked. Sometimes, as he looked at life—the mere current, visible scene—it seemed intensely artistic." [*Financier*, 181]

For Eugene Witla, not a collector or patron but an emerging artist, the beauty was not outside of, but *in* the city, and like Dreiser and Everett Shinn, he was thrilled at its ever present dramatic spectacle. Art becomes, for Witla, part of his discovery of the city, of its grimness and of its humanity. Like the members of the famous Ash-Can Group, a group of eight with "ideals of reality that gave them common cause in painting," [5] Witla believes in the potentialities of beauty in ugliness, and Dreiser, lovingly describing the artist's first canvases, is sharing in this philosophy. It is exciting, for the pictures, as described, are exciting, both for themselves and as part of Witla's passionate interest in his immediate world and his discovery that he can convey his enthusiasm. "He was studying the perspective of his sixteenth New York view,—three engines coming abreast into a great yard of cars. The smoke, the haze, the dingy reds and blues and yellows and greens of kicked about box cars were showing with beauty—the vigor and beauty of raw reality." [192]

Joseph Kwiat, in an article equating Witla and Shinn, observes:

> When Dreiser sympathizes with their [Ash-Can Group] belief in the inherent dignity and character of an honest and living art which portrays every aspect of the city and which seeks for "commonplace beauty" and the possibilities for "beauty in ugliness," Dreiser is also sharing the painters' artistic credo. When Dreiser admires their pictures for their persistence in depicting the city scene with an eye for detail, with directness and brusqueness and power, with raw and undecorated masses, and with solidity of effect, he is also striving for these technical accomplishments in his own fiction. And when Dreiser records the critical controversy . . . he expresses his

awareness of the hazards which confronted those courageous souls who stood firm against the tide of gentility
and fashionableness in favor of an honest and truthful
portrayal of the American scene.[6]

But the greatness of the members of the Ash-Can
Group, of course, as the greatness of Eugene Witla,
was primarily as innovators, as men who opened eyes
"to the then unthought of possibilities in the very
ordinariness around us." [7] One of the leaders of the
group, John Sloan, called the artist "a spectator of
life" and added that he "doesn't need to participate in
adventures." The artist is interested in life the way
God is interested in the universe. This is a good para-
phrase of Witla's principles as depicted in "Youth";
the artist becoming a man who both sees life and
sympathizes with those whom life torments. "This,"
as David Brion Davis notes, "necessitated a fluctua-
tion between an identification with personalities in
specific situations and a retiring, detached perspective
where all life, the evil and ugly, seemed beautiful." [8]

Eugene's growth as an artist, from his clumsy beginnings as a neophyte student to his initial successes as
an illustrator of urban scenes, is carefully detailed, for
it was a subject Dreiser, as a busy magazine editor
and writer, knew and cared a good deal about. From
1895 to 1915 Dreiser wrote many pieces on the themes
of the graphic artist and his task in truthfully portraying city life.[9]

Witla's triumphs as an artist depend, as Robert
Elias points out, "on his ability to view the forces of
life without being subject to them." [10] We see this
ability emerge in "Youth." Leaving Alexandria for
Chicago, Eugene stares out of the train window as the
great city comes in view. First miles of dreary houses,
then factory plants, and then endless railroad tracks.
Engines clanging, trains moving, people waiting at

street crossings—pedestrians, wagon drivers, street
car drivers, drays of beer, trucks of coal, brick, stone,
sand—a spectacle of new, raw, necessary life!" Witla
feels the strength of the city, and like Walt Whitman
he longs to express his awe. "What were these news
paper shadows he had been dealing with in his reading
compared to this vivid, articulate, eager thing? Here
was the substance of a new world, substantial, fasci
nating, different." [17]

As a bill collector in Chicago, young Witla travels
about the city, observing and thrilling to the hectic
world about him:

> He saw scenes that he felt sure he could, when he had
> learned to draw a little better, make great things of,—
> dark, towering factory sites, great stretches of railroad
> yards laid out like a puzzle in rain, snow or bright sun
> light; great smoke-stacks throwing their black height
> athwart morning or evening skies. He liked them best in
> the late afternoon when they stood out in a glow of red
> or fading purple. "Wonderful," he used to exclaim to
> himself, and think how the world would marvel if h
> could ever come to do great pictures like those of Doré
> He admired the man's tremendous imagination. He
> never thought of himself as doing anything in oils or wa
> ter colors or chalk—only pen and ink, and that in great
> rude splotches of black and white. That was the way
> That was the way force was had.
> But he could not do them. He could only think them
> One of his chief joys was the Chicago river, its black
> mucky water churned by puffing tugs and its banks lined
> by great red grain elevators and black coal chutes and
> yellow lumber yards. Here was real color and life—the
> thing to draw; and then there were the low, drab, rain
> soaked cottages standing in lonely, shabby little rows out
> on flat prairie land, perhaps a scrubby tree somewhere
> near. He loved these. He would take an envelope and
> try to get the sense of them—the feel, as he called it—

but it wouldn't come. All he did seemed cheap and commonplace, mere pointless lines and stiff wooden masses.
How did the great artists get their smoothness and
ease? He wondered. [48–49]

He visits galleries and glories in the work of Russian
and French artists, being especially moved by paintings stressing strength and boldness. [50–52] He sees
beauty everywhere. Visiting a girl-friend in a poor
neighborhood on a rainy day, he sees the view as an
artist would.

Looking around here and there one could see in the
open spaces between the houses pools of water standing
in the brown, dead grass. He had crossed a great maze of
black cindered car tracks, where engines and cars were in
great masses, and speculated on the drawings such
scenes would make—big black engines throwing up
clouds of smoke and steam in a gray, wet air; great mazes
of parti-colored cars dank in the rain but lovely. At night
the switch lights in these great masses of yards bloomed
like flowers. He loved the sheer yellows, reds, greens,
blues, that burned like eyes. Here was the stuff that
touched him magnificently, and somehow he was glad
that this raw flowering girl lived near something like
this. [76]

And he sighs, "If I could paint at all I'd like to paint
these things. They're so big and wonderful." [77]
Later, in New York, Eugene took nightly walks.

The city appealed to him, wet or white, particularly the
public squares. He saw Fifth Avenue once in a driving
snowstorm and under sputtering arc lights, and he hur-
ried to his easel next morning to see if he could not put
it down in black and white. It was unsuccessful, or at
least he felt so, for after an hour of trying he threw it
aside in disgust. But these spectacles were drawing him.
He was wanting to do them—wanting to see them
shown somewhere in color. Possible success was a solace

at a time when all he could pay for a meal was fifteen cents and he had no place to go and not a soul with whom to talk. [108-9]

Not only city scenes but city people appealed to Witla. In his studio he worked on a painting of "a mass of East Side working girls flooding the streets after six o'clock. There were dark walls of buildings, a flaring gas lamp or two, some yellow lighted shop windows, and many shaded, half seen faces—bare suggestions of souls and pulsing life." [110]

The city becomes a wondrous place for Eugene as he works on a view of Greeley Square and on one of an L train speeding up the Bowery. "He had an eye for contrasts, picking out lights and shadows sharply, making wonderful flurs that were like colors in precious stones, confused and suggestive." [212] The L train picture is sold to a leading magazine, and he is proud as he studies the excellent reproduction, full of color and life. [114] He has become an artist, and his energy and love has been successfully channeled into important creativity.

Dreiser, in "Youth," traces more than the growth of the artist in Witla. We have a study of a complex, often misguided young man who, unlike Frank Cowperwood, is never quite certain of his potentialities. "Eugene Witla is weak willed, muddled, acutely sensitive, highly introspective." [11] Witla, like the later Augie March, learns that "the world doesn't let hot blood off easy." [12] Early in life he is able to evaluate his parents, a typical middle-class, mildly ambitious small town couple, and his attitude towards them could best be defined as a fond indifference. [15] His indifference extends to the town of Alexandria, and after a brief stint as a printer's boy on the local newspaper Eugene decides that the inhabitants are uninspiring, "a little small, mostly." [29] He longs to get more out of life than Alexandria can provide.

After leaving the Illinois town (much like the teenage heroes of Thomas Wolfe and Sherwood Anderson) he faces Chicago, faces a challenge to his ambitions, to his faith that he is better than others. "This city demanded of you your very best, or it would have little to do with you." [39] He is bullied on his first job and wonders whether he must adjust to the seamier aspects of the city. He decides he must, [42] and he learns to get along in his jobs as stove polisher, real estate assistant, laundry driver, and bill collector.

Witla's perceptions sharpen. He reads a great deal, preferring only realistic literature. [65] He forms opinions on behavior, deciding against rigid adherence to convention and dedicating himself to searching for beauty everywhere. The mansions and large trade buildings seemed cold to him. "He liked, at this time, simple things, simple homes, simple surroundings, the commonplace atmosphere of simple life." [75]

Eugene is as easily depressed as he is elated. [103] He is spoiled by admirers, [153] but he constantly doubts. He is often troubled, and we realize his insecurity which makes his artistic victories all the more impressive. "Youth," like *Winesburg, Ohio* and *Look Homeward Angel*, deserves to be read as a classic study of the young rebel who is caught in a tension between love and hate for American life, love and hate for himself.

"Youth," as well as all of *The "Genius,"* also concerns itself with Witla's sex life, and human nature being what it is, this is what Dreiser's novel is remembered for. The book has achieved historical importance as a result of the famed fight over its suppression, a struggle that ranks with the *Ulysses* case as a pivotal victory in the fight for American literary freedom. The

Executive Secretary of The New York Society for the Suppression of Vice, John Sumner, stated the objections which the puritanic defenders of national decency had for *The "Genius."* He claimed that the Witla saga "reaps the results of his immoral life . . . through the story there are very vivid descriptions of the activities of certain female delinquents who do not, apparently, suffer any ill consequence from their misconduct but, in the language of the day, 'get away with it.' It is wholly conceivable that the reading of such a book by a young woman would be very harmful." [13]

The question of whether *The "Genius"* is lewd and deserving of censorship has long been settled; but the controversy did force critics to face the question of sex in Dreiser's novels, particularly in *The "Genius"* and specifically in the sections pertaining to its influence on Witla's growth as an artist. Randolph Bourne observed that Dreiser deals with the erotic "with an almost religious solemnity," and that it is part of a chaos "not only in the Genius' soul, but in the author's soul, and in America's soul." The real hero of Dreiser's work, according to Bourne, is not Sister Carrie or the Titan or even the Genius, "but that desire within us that pounds in manifold guise against the iron wall of experience. . . . In *The "Genius"* the libido takes the form of an insatiable desire which is sexual and yet incurably aesthetic." Sex becomes the "desire of life." [14]

Art and sex are interwoven themes in the Cowperwood trilogy. At times, for the financier, sex has an almost mystic quality. Cowperwood anticipates Witla in his ability to magnetize women in a remarkably short time. As Cowperwood ages he prefers the artistic minded woman. His preference for Berenice over Aileen demonstrates this.

Witla's interest in women is carefully studied in "Youth," from his early adolescent philanderings in

Alexandria to his more mature operations in Chicago and New York. Dreiser does not gloat nor does he preach; he simply presents and helps us understand how a lonely small-town boy will react during his first freedom away from home. As a boy Witla worshiped school-girls from afar, especially one yellow-haired beauty with dark, burning eyes. At seventeen he meets, attracts, and is rejected by a popular high-school coed, a girl to whom he blurts out his desire to become an artist. "He loved to look out of the window and draw though of late, after knowing Stella so well and coming to quarrel with her because of her indifference, there was little heart in it." [28] The crucial rejection comes during a game of post office.

In Chicago, Witla has his first real affair. "Now, and of a sudden, he was plunged into something which awakened a new, and if not evil, at least disrupting and disorganized propensity of his character. He loved women . . . but his ideal was as yet not clear to him." [44]

While home on a visit Eugene meets his future wife, Angela, and begins a long, increasingly desultory court-ship, which results in trips to her farm home, many quarrels, and a clumsy seduction which leads to mar-riage. While courting Angela, Witla is busily and hap-pily involved with a Chicago artists' model, Ruby Kenny, whom he eventually must rudely reject:

> The artist is a blend of subtleties in emotion which can not be classified. No one woman could have satisfied all sides of Eugene's character at that time. Beauty was the point with him. Any girl who was young, emotional or sympathetic to the right degree and beautiful would have attracted and held him for a while. He loved beauty —not a plan of life. He was interested in an artistic ca-reer, not in the founding of a family. Girlhood—the beauty of youth—was artistic, hence he craved it. [81–82]

In New York, with Angela safely away in Wisconsin torturing herself with thoughts of the one horrible evening, Witla is caught up in bohemian art circles and involved with admiring women, many of whom conveniently prefer a temporary relationship to any thought of marriage. As one comments, "They ought to get a new sex for artists—like they have for worker bees." [154] Miriam Finch, a mother-dominated sculptress, Christina Channing, a famous singer, and Norma Whitmore, an editor and writer, all have affairs with Witla. Dreiser carefully goes into each romance, showing how they exist, in a large part, as compensation for the artist's clumsy, small-town beginnings. The intense Witla, so appealing to New York women, is still very much the Alexandria, Illinois boy who couldn't succeed with the local girls, whose name was rarely called out in the games of post office. Witla grows up in "Youth." But it is a growth that does not come easy. The rest of *The "Genius"* lacks this sense of development, and relapses into a mere chronicle of success, and, what is worse, some of Dreiser's more unenlightened philosophical meanderings on religion and sex. The young Witla is somehow lost.

iii

The "Genius," as the critics have generously pointed out, is not one of Dreiser's more successful works, but the reasons given for the failure are usually limited to hazy references to style and length. The novel falls down for a more definite reason—after the "Youth" section Dreiser was for once unclear about his underlying principles, and as a result many scenes and details float about in an irrelevant way. Dreiser, as usual, was speculating about the nature of American delusions, but his concern for their effects on the artist forced him into a bitter self-analysis which scattered his thinking up too many side-roads. So we have in *The "Genius"* the theme of the materialistic pressures on the artist thrown off balance by an immature concern for the effects of sexual-overindulgence on the creative man. We are never certain whether Eugene Witla's eventual failures are due to sex, whether his passions are, in turn, the result of social patterns he is forced to imitate. However, it is not simply a question of mixed themes, but of too much confusion, too many unconnected theories in a novel whose whole structure demands a single purpose. An artificiality results, especially as we are never satisfied as to whether the "Genius" is a term to be taken at face value or whether there isn't a smirk behind the quotation marks. We never understand whether being a "Genius" (an artist) carries along with its misery a lifetime pass exempting the owner from active participation in his immediate society. Witla, the "Genius," suffers from this indecision on Dreiser's part, and the latter portions of the book, centering as they do on this one figure, fail in proportion to the failure of the chief protagonist.

The working framework of the novel, the introduction of the young man from the country into the urban and political complexities of modern life, has, of course, been successfully utilized by many novelists as the prop for exploring and exposing society's deficiencies. Henry James, Dostoevsky, Stendahl, and Dickens, to mention only four, have used the device of the young man who, in his naïveté, is able to reflect the hypocricies of the new life into which he is injected. The neophyte does this in two ways: by his innocent awareness, and by the changes that occur within his own character. In *The "Genius"* the innocent awareness disappears after the "Youth" section; the later parts of the novel are static.

Dreiser's use of Witla in this regard is comparable to

the role played by Hyacinth in James' *The Princess Casamassima* who, in his unformed but haunted state, felt like a "great square blackboard uninscribed with a stroke of chalk." The city has the same appeal to Hyacinth and Eugene. James' hero was "absorbed in the struggles and sufferings of the millions whose life flowed in the same current as his and who, though they constantly excited his disgust and made him shrink and turn away, had the power to chain his sympathy, to raise it to passion, to convince him for the time at least that real success in the world would be to do something with them and for them." [15] Where James and Dreiser part company is in the use of the central figure. James has Hyacinth primarily set up as a sounding board for the stronger opinions of other protagonists.[16] For Dreiser, however, Witla exists for himself, incorporating in himself the problem of the artist in America, and, while unclear at times about what "goes on," Dreiser sees the corrupting forces as out in the open, unsubtle and certainly not, as James sees them, "irreconcilably . . . beneath the surface."

Though Eugene Witla, in his successes and failures, illustrates various facets of the meeting between the artist and America, Dreiser has unfortunately invested the painter with certain inherent qualities, obviously obtained first hand from the novelist's own experience. Acting in conjunction with Witla's later adventures, they result in a confusion of purpose. And, as I have mentioned, we never understand whether the sex urge serves Witla as a catalyst for his art or is the result of other forces working on him, reducing him to the American stereotype.

Sex, in *The "Genius,"* gradually becomes a symbol for the forces which alternately stimulate and deter the artist. For Witla it is an entangling duality, becoming both the driving force behind his art and the ever seductive image of youth. The sex equals youth equation grows with the novel. "The most dangerous thing to possess a man to the extent of dominating him is an idea. It can and does ride him to destruction. Eugene's idea of the perfection of eighteen was one of the most dangerous things in his nature." [700] It is spelled out for us when Dreiser discusses Witla's changeable nature.

But two things were significant and real—two things to which he was as true and unvarying as the needle to the pole—his love of the beauty of life which was coupled with his desire to express it in color, and his love of beauty in the form of a woman, or rather that of a girl of eighteen. That blossoming of life in womanhood at eighteen!—there was no other thing under the sun like it to him. It was like the budding of the trees in spring; the blossoming of flowers in the early morning; the odor of roses and dew, the color of bright waters and clear jewels. He could not be faithless to that. He could not get away from it. It haunted him like a joyous vision. . . . it remained clear and demanding. He could not escape it—the thought; he could not deny it. He was haunted by this, day after day, and hour after hour; and when he said to himself that he was a fool, and that it would lure him as a will-o'-the-wisp to his destruction and that he could find no profit in it ultimately, still it would not down. The beauty of youth; the beauty of eighteen! To him life without it was a joke, a shabby scramble, a work-horse job, with only silly material details like furniture and houses and steel cars and stores all involved in a struggle for what? To make a habitation for more shabby humanity? Never! To make a habitation for beauty? Certainly! What beauty? The beauty of old age? Nonsense! The beauty of maturity? No! The beauty of youth? Yes. The beauty of eighteen. No more and no less. That was the standard, and the history of the world proved it. Art, literature, romance, history, poetry—if they did not turn on this and the lure of this

and the wars and the sins because of this, what did they
turn on? He was for beauty. The history of the world
justified him. Who could deny it? [295]

Though we can question the exclamation points we
cannot doubt the sincerity. Witla's final extra-marital
affair, his intense relationship with Suzanne Dale,
brings this desperate search for identification with
youth to a climax. Again using romantic, yet curiously
proper images, Dreiser describes Witla's sensations. "If
wet roses could outrival a maiden in all her freshness,
he thought he would like to see it. Nothing could equal
the beauty of a young woman in her eighteenth or
nineteenth year." [522] His art, he tells Suzanne,
seems to come back through her. He has discovered
what he feels is the source of his artistic powers as he
cries out, "I love youth! I love beauty!" [587]
For Witla, Suzanne's particularly young mind and
body seemed to embody all the qualities of the per-
fect woman. He justifies the seduction to Suzanne's
mother by explaining that "she's finer than the whole
current day conception of society and life." [618]
Dreiser, as we have noted, saw America as being at
middle-age, filled with distorted visions, and his artist,
as a primary reflector of society, therefore must embody this concept. Desiring youth, Witla, like Mark
Twain, could combine a fervid desire for former un-
spoiled days with a despair for the present and a slight
hope for the future, but a future to be somehow saved
by the strength of youth. Witla's parade of women, ac-
curately pegged by F. O. Matthiessen as "abstract
monsters of unreality," [17] thus comes to a logical end
with Suzanne—young, spirited, unformed, the rich,
potential American Galatea who could be molded as
she is loved.
Balanced against Suzanne and the other nonlegal

women in Witla's crowded life is his wife, Angela (the "angel"), the tormented, uncomprehensive woman, who, as we have noted, is, like Dreiser's first wife, a bit older than her husband and the supposed agent for ruining Witla's life by serving as a too willing and over-responsive sexual partner. Dreiser believed that one's sexual life could "distort the sense of color, weaken that balanced judgment of character which is so essential to a normal interpretation of life, make all striving hopeless, take from art its most joyous conception, make life itself seem unimportant and death a relief." [246]

The book is filled with repeated sermons on this topic: over and over, with the uniform persistency of an army training film, the point is made that art and abstinence go hand in hand. Even Angela believes this distortion. She had heard the back-fence oracles in her home town discuss the matter, and consequently she was determined not to encourage Eugene too much in his "animal passions." But she also realized that sex was her primary hold on an elusive husband, and when Eugene announces he is going off with Suzanne the dazed, unhappy wife throws open her robe and stands naked before the shocked artist-husband in a final effort to revive his interest and fully realize his love. Sex, like youth, was not enough by itself to inspire Dreiser's American artist. And as Henry Adams could observe from his cold vantage point, American society regarded the victory over sex as its greatest triumph.

It is Angela who created the "Genius" myth which Witla comes to accept. It serves as both the explanation for her love and the alibi for his periods of unfaithfulness. Witla never doubts the accuracy of the label, believing he is not an ordinary man and not slated for an ordinary life. Other figures in the novel back up this insight. One of his magazine employers tells him that all "Geniuses" are erratic, and Suzanne announces she loves him because he is a "Genius" and can do anything he pleases. Thus Witla, the American artist, is excused, by the very nature of his talents, from a certain amount of social responsibility. This viewpoint runs through a number of Dreiser's essays, coming at times in direct conflict with his overall view of a corrupt society needing drastic, immediate improvement. It is a dilemma Dreiser never came to terms with. The artist is the first to understand the all-embracing corruption about him, yet, as a citizen removed from his contemporaries, he is not in a position of action. Perhaps, by definition he can never be a part of the society he paints and is somewhat like the paradoxical figure in Norman Mailer's *Barbary Shore* who laments about the modern revolutionary "who seeks to create a world in which he would find it intolerable to live." [18] The artist resists societal pressures yet feels a need to understand and clarify what is about him. I would like to suggest that at each point in his writing where Dreiser is conscious of playing the artist, a man of talent, he loses his great natural sympathy for his characters and his writing lapses into a limpid artificiality.

Eugene Witla, as he changes from the raw, yearning youth to the renowned artist is led astray, not only by sex, love of youth, and a belief in his "Genius"; his primary defection is his ultimate acceptance of the money-conscious criteria imposed on him. He states this quite bluntly. "I can't live by painting pictures as I am living by directing magazines. Art is very lovely. I am satisfied to believe I am a great painter. Nevertheless I made little out of it, and since then I have learned to live. It's sad, but it's true." [518] Learning to live means, for Witla, wealth, power, position—all that teased and destroyed Hurstwood and Clyde Griffith. This is the threat to the American artist as seen in

the Witla story, that he will become a conformist in
an atmosphere where conformity is unable to produce
a truthful art. It is the same weakness that H. L.
Mencken observed in Dreiser himself:

"The truth about Dreiser is that he is still in the
transition stage between Christian Endeavor and civi-
lization, between Warsaw, Indiana, and the Socratic
grove, between being a good American and being a
free man, and so he sometimes vacillates perilously between a moral sentimentalism and a somewhat ex-
travagant revolt." [19]

R. L. Duffus observed that "some artists escape
from reality, some into it. Dreiser was necessarily of the
latter group." [20] Witla was, in his best moments, an
escaper into reality. The irony, of course, comes when
the artist is seduced by the forces he wants to portray
on canvas. The strength and viciousness of these forces
are made clearer as Witla assumes favorable positions
in the publishing field. One successful office is described as "a bear-garden, a den of prizefighters, liars,
cutthroats and thieves in which every man was for
himself openly and avowedly and the devil take the
hindmost." [424] The boss, in another office in which
Witla works, continually equates life and business.
"Life is a constant condition of readjustment, and
every good business man knows it." [465] In order to
survive and live in a world of glitter there was the necessity of daily battle, an intensification of and depar-
ture from the life in Witla's birthplace of Alexandria,
Illinois, where his father (Thomas Jefferson Witla)
sold sewing machines in a community dedicated to
hard work and thrift. Eugene, in his restless early life,
rejects Alexandria, and his family quite naturally become peripheral to his more important interests. In
moments of loneliness Witla becomes nostalgic, making open declarations of favor of the home town virtues

from which he fled. But the return and redemption is not for him.

Dreiser's protagonists seldom reach a satisfactory adjustment, but in *The "Genius"* the novelist inches towards a possible answer in terms of religious acceptance. After a bout with Christian Science, Witla finally lapses into a state of "philosophic open-mindedness. . . . He came to know that he did not know what to believe. All apparently was permitted, nothing fixed." [726] Angela dies giving birth to their child and Witla finds contentment in this living result of his unfortunate marriage. Like Papa Gerhardt (in *Jennie Gerhardt*) his hope becomes fused in the younger generation which is as yet uncorrupted. The book ends with Witla lost in speculations about the infinite wonders of the world: "Great art dreams welled up in his soul as he viewed the sparkling deeps of space." [736] It is a personal evasion clouded with mysticism, but it is the only possible ending for a confused book and an unsure character based, as we have noted, on a composite of three men. The amalgamation was an unhappy one, Dreiser's portrayal of the forces detrimental to the artist becomes unsure, and this lack of a steady, firm concept forces the book into meaningless probings. Dreiser's forceful honesty and bold enthusiasm is far from enough. Like most truthful novelists, Dreiser never gives us a complete answer, but in his major works we are at least given a clearer understanding of the basic troubles which are the *raison d'être* of the novels, and we are given characters whose suffering becomes real. If all of *The "Genius"* had the force and direction of its "Youth" section, perhaps the novel would deserve to be what John Cowper Powys called it, "the Prose-Iliad of the American Scene." It is Dreiser's greatest failure as it showed Dreiser's greatest promise.

4 THE BULWARK
AMERICAN RELIGION AND
THE AMERICAN DREAM

> If I were to preach any doctrine to the world it would
> be love of change, or at least lack of fear of it. From the
> Bible I would quote: "The older order changeth, giving
> place to the new," and from Nietzsche: "Learn to revalue
> your values." The most inartistic and discouraging phase of
> the visible scene, in so far as it relates to humanity, is its
> tendency to stratification, stagnation and rigidity. Yet from
> somewhere, fortunately, . . . there blows ever and anon a
> new breath, quite as though humanity were an instrument
> through which a force were calling for freshness and
> change. The old or unyielding die or crumble; the unwitting
> young arise to take their place.
>
> THEODORE DREISER
> "Change"

"THE BULWARK" (1946), Dreiser's slow and mannered
study of the spiritual struggles of a modern American
Quaker, is a disturbing book for most critics. The
usual cliches about Dreiser's awkwardness, lengthiness,
and love of details cannot be utilized, for none of them
seem to apply to this strange novel. It is as if Dreiser
had to be judged anew.

The book opens late in the nineteenth century.
Solon Barnes and Benecia Wallin are being married in
a Friends' meetinghouse at Dukla, Pennsylvania. A
sense of brooding profoundness is given us, and we are

given to understand, right off, that there is a conflict present between the old-fashioned, hard-rock Quaker fundamentalist ways of life and the new, success-oriented ideas which attract the younger Friends.

> Although a moderate proportion of the men and women present were arrayed in a modification of that earlier costume and manner, many of the others were more modern in aspect, even though they were far from having the current fashions.
>
> The older men were beardless, and most of them retained the simple dress of their predecessors, the roll-less coat collar and smooth, pocketless coat front and round, wide-brimmed black hat; the women of the older group wore the traditional plain Quaker bonnet and sober black cape or shawl, over a full, ankle-length gray skirt, and gray bodice with white neckerchief—favoring, in addition, a very plain, broad, flat shoe and very small gray stringlike ribbons under their chins, to keep their bonnets on. If there were no smart suits or dresses as we understand the term today, neither were there any dull or slovenly modifications of them.
>
> On the other hand the younger of both sexes, in many instances, had gone so far in their concession to the enormous spirit of change and modernity that had overwhelmed Quakerism as to lay aside almost entirely those outward signs of an inward and spiritual grace.[1]

This overwhelming spirit of change becomes the essence of the action of *The Bulwark*, the struggle between the old and the new, a struggle that changes Solon from "a Quaker who progresses from a point of view that interprets the Book of Discipline with an orthodox and determined severity to a point of view that enables him to assert tolerance and love for all created things."[2] It is a story of conflict, paralleling the story of a man's growth through disillusionment, a process leading inevitably to an almost "unmitigated tragedy." [3] At the end of the novel, as Edmund Wilson observes, one gradually finds himself "won over by the candor and humanity of the author, then finally . . . moved by a powerful dramatic pathos which Dreiser has somehow built up." [4] This "somehow" is not arrived at haphazardly. It is a result of the careful building up of the action along with the gradual, careful emergence of Solon Barnes' character. We learn of Solon through the action, and the action, in turn, hinges on Solon's strength and on his discoveries.

There is another aspect of *The Bulwark* which helps to explain its success. Despite the apparent simplicity of the book, which led one critic to call it "largely lifeless; its drama undeveloped," [5] we do get to know Solon Barnes and the Quaker world he lived with. F. O. Matthiessen, noting the lack of Dreiser's usual massive documentation, believes the novel reads like a chronicle and is far more a "symbolic than naturalistic novel, basically as bare as a parable." [6]

The Bulwark is certainly bare, yet, oddly enough, bereft of the multitude of details we associate with Dreiser's other works, it gives us what many of Dreiser's other novels lack—a sense of historical mood. One critic has pointed out that Dreiser "seems to have no way of writing out of a certain time-place spirit which is so strong that it pervades and breaks down everything else." [7] Perhaps this is because Dreiser too often speaks from a soapbox perched over the scene he is describing, or perhaps it is because of his personal involvement with so much of his writing, an involvement that often leads to self-confession. For as Ludwig Lewisohn has observed, "Dreiser's work . . . like the work of other and greater writers, like Goethe's and Tolstoi's, are [sic] one long confession." [8] But in any case *The Bulwark*, with its simple but solid portrayal of Quaker life, does give us a strong sense of place that reinforces the action of social conflict and the parallel story of a man's growth.

ii

It is, indeed, "a very old fashioned America that reasserts itself in *The Bulwark*," [9] one that begins by being certain of its values and ends by re-examining them. We have a picture of an older generation "from its own point of view" [10] and we then see this point of view exposed to temptation after temptation, shock after shock. To quote the dust jacket: "The essential conflict . . . lies in the problem of a devout Quaker whose life and beliefs are shattered by the materialism of twentieth-century America. Because he fails to understand the new generation Solon Barnes sees in the worldliness of his own children a questioning of his faith."

This is the action, tending almost, as Harry M. Campbell overstates, to an "epicureanism infused into Quaker sobriety," and leading, most certainly, to a tragedy which we are adequately prepared for by "subtle fore-shadowings." [11] The fore-shadowing begins with the already quoted description of Solon's wedding. After this introduction the story line drops back to a description of Solon's strict Quaker parents, and from then on the novel has a straight chronological development, following Solon from a mother-dominated boyhood, through his marriage, and finally to his tragic relations with his children.

Solon's father, Rufus Barnes, moved from Maine to New Jersey a few years after his son's birth, and through inheritance and hard work becomes a worldly success. He moves his family into an old mansion which he redecorates. Noticing the decayed condition of his land surrounding the large house, Rufus Barnes dreams of ways to restore it to its former beauty, not for sinful purposes but for decent appreciation. But it is a description of the renovated house, given early in the novel, that prepares us for future action:

> And in the center of what was once no doubt a large smooth lawn to the south of the house, he saw the remains of a double circle of decayed posts so arranged as to indicate the one-time presence of an arched-over and exceptionally large arbor or garden-party retreat such as still existed on other superior estates of this area. Either grapes or flowering vines had, most likely, provided the shelter from the sun here. Hence this arbor suggested something which never before had in any way intruded itself in Rufus's life: leisure, the assembling of people of means under such circumstances as precluded all thought of ordinary labor such as he had been forced to do. It suggested plenty and also waste in the matter of food, drink, clothing, and show, which he was convinced should not be—never in this house at least. For why, he thought, could not such beauty and charm be divorced from waste and show, to say nothing of greed, drunkenness, immorality, and the other sins of living which George Fox and the faith he proclaimed had so valiantly sought to put aside forever? [8]

Thus Solon inherits not only a house and a life of comfort (Solon's married life is spent in the home of his childhood), but he inherits a built-in problem that restates itself in many forms throughout the novel: Can one accept the rewards of commercial success and still be a devout Quaker? Like his father, Solon sees the evil clearly but, also like his father, he is forced into constant compromises which, on careful examination, appear to be hypocritical and self-defeating.

Solon, a quiet, determined boy, often accompanied his father on routine business trips around the growing farm community, trips resulting in financial advancement: "Because of the selling phase . . . he was slowly and surely compelled to see the need of better clothing and the value of a fast horse and good buggy, all of which gave him an air of prosperity and well-being." [25] As Solon becomes involved in a world of commerce he hardens as a Quaker, asking divine guidance and waiting for the Inner Light. We see Solon develop to resemble his father, a man "whose grateful religious mood . . . ran side by side with the practical." [27] Only it seems that Solon is stronger than his father, a better Quaker and a better businessman.

Compromise follows compromise, each bringing new tensions. The Quaker Book of Disciplines states under the heading Trade: "When any become possessed of ample means, they should remember that they are duly stewards who must render an account for the right use of the things committed to their care." How, wonders Solon, can one profess Quakerism and lead, at the same time, a life whose goals are aimed at worldly success.

Solon moves ahead to a position in a Philadelphia bank, a flourishing institution largely controlled by his future father-in-law, Justus Wallin, a rich man impressed by the young Quaker's soundness, industry, modesty, and business intelligence. Wallin, like Rufus Barnes, has to square his Quaker beliefs with his business life. His answer is a happy rationalization. His wealth came from the Lord and was intended to be an instrument for the general good. On occasion, Wallin would rise at a meeting of the Friends, and testify to this belief. But despite his many good deeds, some of his fellow Quakers were skeptical, wondering whether Wallin's stewardship of God's materials "might not necessarily require the amount of wealth he was accumulating." [40, 47]

The Wallin household puzzles Solon, impressing him with the "problem of wealth as opposed to simplicity." [56] His mother secretly wonders whether the Wallins' great wealth may not, in truth, be a heavy spiritual handicap. Solon is awed by Wallin's bank with its rich decorations. He has, by now, successfully courted Benecia Wallin, and so is drawn to the Wallin household.

> After that it seemed to follow naturally that Solon should spend alternate week ends at the Wallin home in Dukla. This meant going against the Quaker custom which prescribed that those who make or admit of proposals of marriage to each other should not dwell in the same house from the time they begin to be so interested. Still, the Wallins, like many other Friends, were inclined to a milder interpretation of these older and sterner commandments. [96]

At the marriage there were those "who had discarded the Quaker habit . . . nevertheless to hold to the faith in most of its commands." And there were those who were "straining at the leash and parents who were grieved by no longer strictly conforming children." As Solon and Benecia leave the service they are greeted by an "un-Quakerish shower of rice and old shoes." [98, 100] The first part of the novel ends with the wedding, with its purpose made more than clear, its action stated and restated. In almost Aristotelian precision we are given the Purpose of the drama to follow. The Passion and Perception are inevitable.

At the end of *The "Genius"* Dreiser, in one of his lamentable bursts of kindergarten metaphysics, attempts to define religion:

> If I were to personally define religion I would say that it is a bandage that man has invented to protect a soul made bloody by circumstance; an envelope to pocket him from the unescapable and unstable illimitable. We seek to think of things as permanent and see them so.

Religion gives life a habitation and a name apparently—
though it is an illusion. So we are brought back to time
and space and illimitable mind—as what? And we shall
always stand before them attributing to them all those
things which we cannot know. [734]

In *The Bulwark* religion becomes more than an illusion. For Barnes, religion is a guide and a way of life.
He is a decent man, he lives by the admirable Quaker
precepts, and he naturally expects his children to do
likewise. Unfortunately, Solon does not understand the
danger signs, the warnings of change which are obvious to the reader. He is not a stupid man, and he certainly is unlike the flabby hero of Ford Madox Ford's,
The Good Soldier, who is supremely unaware of what
is really happening. Rather, Solon is aware of trouble,
is bothered by the show of wealth around him, but
fails to comprehend the attitudes that go along with it.
His father-in-law has generously provided a large, elaborate home for the newly married couple. The luxury
bothers Solon and he discusses the matter with his
wife who comforts him by pointing out that now that
they possess money it will be possible "to do many
things which will help us to feel that the use of what
has been given us is not unacceptable to God." [104]

But it is more than wealth or an obvious conspicu-
ous consumption. An American social revolution is in
full swing, bringing new insights and new standards
for the younger generation. Though apparently isolated, the Barnes children are susceptible to the indirect controls of the commercial world, a commercial
world making the most of the undisciplined leisure
time of many of its inhabitants.

Solon, advancing to important positions in his bank,
is pleased at the institution's growth, yet "he was becoming more and more mentally disturbed as to where
lay the dividing line between ambition and an irreli-

gious greed, between the desire for power and wealth and a due regard for Quaker precepts." [113] The son of one of Solon's Quaker friends, a boy whom Solon placed in a trusted position in the bank, is caught stealing in order to pay for women and other worldly pleasures. "His excuse was that his father was so severe with him, his home life so narrow, that he could not resist the temptation to embark on a freer, happier existence." [117] Solon tries to offer his sympathies to the father, but his attempts fail, just as he will fail, later on, to understand his own children.

The five Barnes children, Isobel, Dorothea, Etta, Orville, and Stewart, all show signs of rebelling at an early age.

> The Barnes children, although unwittingly enough at first, were becoming, as they grew older, more and more of a problem, for each one in turn could not help being confronted by the marked contrast between the spirit of the Barnes home and that of the world at large. In spite of the many admirable qualities of the home, these were distinctly at variance with the rush and swing and spirit of the time itself, and this fact could scarcely fail to impress even the least impressionable minds. Isobel had already noticed many things in connection with her home which were not common elsewhere. Her parents and most of their friends dressed and acted so formally. People in the outside world were not so, as she had already observed. They laughed more, conducted themselves more easily. [138]

America was speeding up, many Quakers even purchasing motorcars and whizzing about the countryside. Each child understands that, for some reason, he is not able to participate in this fast, fascinating life. The youngest boy, Steward, was "sick and tired of hearing about the Inner Light." For "Its impact, as far as he was concerned, was purely imaginary." He wants a good time, and he believes the Quakers are out of touch with "real life," [195] the life so vividly described in various publications read on the sly at a local bookshop. Etta, too, desires a "brighter world." Orville, a calm, objective manipulator, does not openly rebel, yet in his calculated, opportunistic way he becomes a parody of the Quaker principles of honesty and decency. Isobel, a homely girl, is also a victim of the world she is denied, for she is constantly aware of her social ineptitudes, a failure magnified by the Quaker way of life.

Etta leaves home, under the influence of a bohemian girl-friend, and moves to Greenwich Village. Dorothea enters the social world, and under the guidance of a society-minded aunt, marries well and lives a life Solon can never understand. Orville becomes a business success and a prig. Isobel lives a life of quiet frustration. All are spiritually and painfully estranged from their parents, but the tragedy comes to focus in terms of Stewart, the child with the most potentiality. A wild boy, he is sent away to school and takes up with a fast crowd. On one of their sojourns to a nearby city they meet some forward girls and Stewart is asked to help in the seduction of one of the new acquaintances. Unknown to the boys the girl has a weak heart, and the administration of a drug (slipped into her drink) causes her death. The boys panic, leave her by the highway, and are quickly arrested and charged with murder. Overcome with shame, Stewart commits suicide in prison, the supreme victim of the tension between the family and the society. A relative, attempting to console Solon, puts the blame on society. "Remember . . . things have changed since we were all children together. There are so many diversions and temptations that we had no knowledge of when we were young." [297]

Solon is broken. He finally understands how far away his children had grown from him. "Indeed, for all their socially prominent and respectable lives, never had they shown the least interest in the religion that was sacred to him. On the contrary, how intense was their interest in the automobile, the country club, the whole round of parties and dances and entertainments which made up the worldly life they had chosen." [325–26]

A repentant Etta, returning from New York City, watches over her father till his death. After the funeral she breaks out sobbing. Orville is angry, for he feels her evil reputation was part of the family humiliation. Etta shakes her head. "Oh, I am not crying for myself, or for Father—I am crying for life." [337] Life has failed Solon, not only in terms of his children but in terms of his business. As he grows older he is increasingly disturbed by what he considers sharp, borderline banking practices, and he even goes so far as to secretly report his own bank to a federal investigating agency. Finally, unable to reconcile his religion with the financial practices of his banking associates, Solon dramatically resigns from the bank in which he labored for so many years. His fellow directors are hurt and puzzled, although they have always admired Solon. Previously, they had adopted a rather patronizing attitude toward Solon's religion. "Yes," one of the directors once commented, with a nod to Solon's office, "it's interesting, the way these Quakers stick to their principles. They seem shrewd enough to make money, though." [221]

The Book of Discipline states, "In all our dealings and transactions among men, strict justice should be observed, and no motives of pecuniary interest should induce any of our members to impose upon others." Solon, in the end, comes to accept this idea fully, making no more compromises. As a fellow director remarks after Solon's resignation, "And he's not altogether wrong. . . . The only trouble with his principles is that they're too high for these days." [305] It has reached a point where the unalloyed goodness of pure Christianity could not fit into American life. It was compromise or perish.

iii

Percy Lubbock, writing of Balzac, stated that the French novelist "was almost too prosaic for the creation of virtue," [12] and undoubtedly this states a problem crucial to Dreiser and especially to *The Bulwark*. For while he develops the conflict between Solon Barnes' religion and the pressures of American life, he must, at the same time, show us the growth of an essentially virtuous man, a protagonist who is both good and unperceptive.

Dreiser has always managed to create sympathy for his characters, as Granville Hicks notes.

We must say a word about Dreiser's humanitarianism. During his lifetime he supported a variety of causes, and, whatever mistakes he may have made, his indignation against injustice did rest firmly on his sense of the dignity of the individual human being. There are no contemptible persons in Dreiser's novels. Although at times he professed a Nietzschean scorn of the masses . . . he instinctively made the best case possible for any person he wrote about. Perhaps one reason why he made Solon Barnes a Quaker is that the Friends have always been the most generously humanitarian of the Christian sects.[13]

There might have been personal reasons for Dreiser's special concern for Solon; Mrs. Dreiser believed Solon Barnes was, in essence, a study of Dreiser's father. "Only, his father had been not merely a confirming religionist but a narrow one, who, according to

Theodore, demanded that his children follow blindly the tenets of the church." [14] And Robert Elias, writing of *The Bulwark*, feels that "Solon undergoes a change in character that transforms him into a person whose attitudes clearly reflect Dreiser's own." [15] For, like Dreiser himself, Solon is indeed "a man with much sweetness." The story of Barnes, according to Dreiser, was one "I have carried in mind for many, many years —all of thirty." [16]

Solon's growth is as carefully chronicled as are the problems he faces. He was an overprotected child, catered to by his mother and aunt, the latter who "was very fond of the boy, by reason of his quiet and thoughtful demeanor, his absorbing love for his mother, and his apparent freedom from vanity in any form." [13] Solon was devoted to his mother, who "in her sober, religious, laboring way . . . had always made much of him—her only boy. He was, as she could see since first he began to babble and play, not as active mentally or as inventive as some babies she had seen." [14] When Solon was seven he received a serious injury to his ankle, and his mother, believing he was near death, prayed for God to spare her son's life.

> And after that his mother's sincerity and goodness and her desire for his welfare, as well as his debt to her, seemed to become an ever present thing to him. He desired never, either in her presence or absence, to do anything that he felt she might not approve of. Always she seemed to come first in his thoughts, and yet throughout her life and his, in so far as the two paralleled each other, he indulged in exceedingly few expressions of his deep affection and regard. She knew always, he was sure, that he cared for her as she would wish him to care, and she in return felt the same in regard to him. [20]

Solon was a strong, peaceful boy; when teased, however, he would be able to handle himself, and as a

Quaker he was often teased for his "thees" and "thous." Once he defeated a local bully who continually mocked him. But most of his childhood was centered at home, and over his bed was the motto: "The earth is the Lord's and the fullness thereof." Solon was obviously not overly intelligent, and "he was not temperamentally inclined toward the higher phases of education in any form." [30] He was rather good at mathematics but lacking in literature, a subject controlled by the strict surveillance of the Friends' school he attended. He had a good business sense and thrilled at being allowed to keep his father's cashbooks.

Solon was obviously isolated from the American scene. A local social quarrel, involving the issue of whether or not to close down the local red-light district, didn't bother him. "In Solon's case, having heard so much concerning good and evil as words, and having personally seen so little of evil in the form here displayed, he could not possibly look back of the surface appearance to the less obvious forces of ignorance, poverty, and the lack of such restraining and yet elevating influences as had encompassed his own life . . . to him, all those who had so sinned were thoroughly bad, their souls irredeemable." [35] As he advanced into business, life became "a series of law governed details, each one of which had the import of being directly connected with the divine will. Honesty was a thing commanded by God." [90] Solon is distressingly trusting and naïve, once coming upon a robbery and unwittingly being tricked into aiding the wrong man.

Along with his wife the prospering Solon and his growing family are considered "symbols of communal respectability and prosperity."

The Barnes were well-to-do; they were Quakers, and they were kind and courteous to everyone. Though Solon had no graces of speech, no artifices by which the attention of the crowd is attracted and fixed, he was liked by the intelligent and discerning in all walks of life. He was praised for his fairness to his employees, commended for his willingness to contribute to all worthy cases of poverty or distress, and favorably thought of by the members of Dukla meeting. He was a good man—one of the nation's bulwarks. [124]

After Stewart's tragic death in prison his wife reflects on Barnes' character over their married life. "For twenty years, in connection with all sorts of matters, public and private, in sickness and in health, in season and out of season, she had yet to see him lose his temper, burst forth in unseemly wrath, or do anything which she considered unfair or unkind." [167] Solon finds comfort in his Quaker books during his final days. His essential characteristics of strength, belief, coupled with a not overshrewd intelligence, lead him to naïve speculations on great, eternal problems. He dies believing "God talks directly to man when his help is needed and man asks Him for it—He does not fail him." [333–34] Religion provides, as always, comfort, but it certainly does not provide the perception needed to raise his children, to cope with modern life, or to successfully conduct business in the American manner.

Much nonsense has been written equating Dreiser's personal philosophies with the statements of the chief characters in his novels. This is especially true of those who would see, in Solon's unswerving religious devotions, a reflection of Dreiser's ideas—the point being that Dreiser, the clumsy naturalist, had finally come to his senses. Not only is this a wonderful example of the "intentional fallacy" at work, it also fails to understand Dreiser's great concern for the characters he creates; because Dreiser understands Solon Barnes does not, per se, mean that he agrees with him. To quote Hicks again: "Dreiser was Dreiser and not the exemplar of some theory. He was the lost, bewildered man of the turn of the century, caught between the economics of monopoly capitalism and the economics of small-scale competition. With the most painful honesty he set forth the dilemmas of his generation and, by stating what he knew about men, said something about man." [17]

Hicks is right. *The Bulwark* certainly says something about man, about religion, and about America. It is an important novel based on contradictions in the American ethic—and the problem it studies is not limited to the Quaker faith or to an earlier America.

AN AMERICAN TRAGEDY
THE DREAM, THE FAILURE, AND
THE HOPE

> Our most outstanding phases, of course, are youth, opti-
> mism and illusion. These run through everything we do,
> affect our judgments and passions, our theories of life. As
> children we should all have had our fill of these, and yet
> even at this late date . . . it is difficult for any of us to
> overcome them. Still, no one can refuse to admire the
> youth and optimism of America, however much they may
> resent its illusion. There is always something so naïve about
> its method of procedure, so human and tolerant at times;
> so loutish, stubborn and ignorantly insistent at others.
>
> THEODORE DREISER
> "Some Aspects of National Character"

"AN AMERICAN TRAGEDY" (1925) is Dreiser's most ambitious novel, telling, through the history of Clyde
Griffiths, of the hopes and failures of the American
dream. The failure of the family unit, as chronicled in
Jennie Gerhardt; the failure of the business ethic, as
told in the Cowperwood trilogy; the failure of religion,
as related in *The Bulwark*—all these themes come together in the long novel of the short life of an American boy.

As Dreiser's most important work, it has met with
the most critical attention. It is a work that, even today, challenges and offends many contemporary crit-

ics. J. Donald Adams of the *New York Times Book Review* still regards the novel with horror as the representative of all that went wrong with the naturalists, men who "have tended to keep their characters on the animal plane." Adams devoted part of two columns to abusing *An American Tragedy*. Dreiser, he tells us, "scanted, as all the naturalists do, the element of moral conflict without which no great fiction can be written, for he fobbed the whole wretched business off on that scapegoat of our time, society." And Dreiser, according to Adams, was not only a clumsy writer, he was "ignorant" and "befuddled." [1]

The same attack, on a slightly higher level, is made by the eminent Hawthorne scholar, Randall Stewart, in a recent essay which telegraphs its intent in its didactic title "Dreiser and the Naturalistic Heresy." Naturalists, we are informed, are amoral because they assume man is a puppet. "In the naturalistic view, then, man is ruled by forces from without, or forces from within, or both." *An American Tragedy* is the "most completely naturalistic of all American novels." Therefore, by definition, it is an amoral book. Dreiser, despite his compassion, "moving power," and "exciting impact"; despite the fact that Stewart grants he "has presented before our very eyes the American experience in such raw, astounding bulk"; despite his having done justice "to the tremendous forces which play upon us"; and despite the novelist's having "recounted our failures with such tender extenuation"—despite all this he is to be blamed, for "Clyde is not responsible, in the last analysis, because he didn't make himself. And this, I fear, is the gospel according to Theodore Dreiser." [2] It is certainly not, the critic makes painfully evident, the gospel according to Randall Stewart.

This is in the ancient tradition of Dreiser criticism, revised and prettied up for contemporary consumption.

?aul Elmer More, Stuart P. Sherman, and Robert
Shafer made basically the same observations. Shafer,
'or example, called *An American Tragedy* "a tale of
human irresponsibility, supported by youthful preju-
dices never relinquished, built up on false antitheses;
and capped by a merely circumstantial realism calculated to give the narrative a deceptive air of importance." *An American Tragedy*, Shafer feels, is a failure
because Dreiser is a naturalist. "His difficulty is that
his mechanistic naturalism compels him so to select
and manipulate facts of experience as to deny, through
his narrative, that human life has any meaning or
value. The attempt is suicidal." [3]

These serious criticisms often border on the hysteri-
cal, as when J. Donald Adams calls Dreiser's influence
on contemporary American novelists "negative," and
"destructive." [4] A careful study of *An American Tragedy*, the chosen battlefield for most of the attacks, will
show, however, that this brilliantly constructed novel
is far from a moronic hymn of despair, that it is not, as
William Lyon Phelps would have us believe, a book
following "the fortunes of a nincompoop from childhood to chair." [5] It is a warm exciting novel, a book
about the believable anguish of a confused boy in a
changing, confusing America.

ii

An American Tragedy does have many of the
familiar Dreiserian rough spots, so adequately described by H. L. Mencken.

I spent the better part of forty years trying to induce him
to reform and electrify his manner of writing, but so far
as I am aware with no more effect than if I had sought
to persuade him to take up golf or abandon his belief in
non-Euclidian arcana. The defects of his style, of course,
have been somewhat exaggerated by a long line of liter-

ary popinjays, including myself; he was quite capable, on occasion, of writing simply and even gracefully, as you will discover if you turn to Chapter XIII of Book III of the present tale. Nevertheless, his was predominantly viscous writing, and not infrequently its viscosity was increased by clichés and counter-words that pulled up the reader in an extremely painful manner.[6]

The most appalling defect is Dreiser's failure to capture the speech patterns of the wealthy protagonists he deals with in the latter sections of the novel. As F. O. Matthiessen has pointed out, "we have no illusion that we are listening to possible talk."[7] Certainly such bits of upper-class badinage as "Did you hear who is being touted for stroke next year over at Cornell?"[8] would have given F. Scott Fitzgerald the fantods; and Sondra Finchley's baby talk, "Whatever matter wissum sweet today? Face all dark. Cantum be happy out here wis Sondra and all these nicey good-baddies?" [593] makes one wonder whether Clyde didn't take the wrong girl for a rowboat ride.

Many of the clumsy passages, as usual, can be blamed on Dreiser's sophomoric attempts at moralizing and philosophizing. The opening paragraph of Chapter xlv of Book ii is a good example. Clyde has been contemplating the murder of Roberta.

There are moments when in connection with the sensitively imaginative or morbidly anachronistic—the mentality assailed and the same not of any great strength and the problem confronting it of sufficient force and complexity—the reason not actually toppling from its throne, still totters or is warped or shaken—the mind befuddled to the extent that for the time being, at least, unreason or disorder and mistaken or erroneous counsel would appear to hold against all else. In such instances the will and the courage confronted by some great difficulty which it can neither master nor endure, appears in some to recede in precipitate flight, leaving only panic and temporary unreason in its wake. [500]

In describing district attorney Mason, Dreiser remarks on his ugliness which "resulted in what the Freudians are accustomed to describe as a psychic sex scar." [547] And we have such sentences as: "So, by virtue of such mental prestidigitation and tergiversation, inspired and animated as it was by his desire for Sondra, his inability to face the facts in connection with Roberta, he achieved the much-coveted privilege of again seeing her, over one week-end at least, and in such a setting as never before in his life had he been privileged to witness." [480]

Dreiser, at times, is a language show-off. He mentions a "circumambient atmosphere of suspicion," [542] and Roberta's fear that her pregnancy will be discovered is described as the "stigma of unsanctioned concupiscence." [402] To deny Dreiser's occasional awkwardness would be stupid; but to dismiss the novel because of these flaws would be even more absurd.

iii

An American Tragedy contains more than Dreiser's often mentioned compassion; it is a novel of artistry, in its theme as well as its structure. There are three sections to the work; the first describing Clyde's childhood and early youth in Kansas City; the second recounting his later struggles, ending with the murder; and the third telling of his trial and execution. Each book reveals a different stage in Clyde's development and awareness, and each begins with the possibility of hope and ends in tragedy and despair. The entire book is framed by two similar scenes, opening with Clyde and his missionary parents proselytizing on a summer's night in a city street and closing with an almost identical scene in another city, with Clyde's nephew, Rus-

sell, taking his place. The obviously contrived envelope
is used by Dreiser to show the continuous nature of the
tragedy, in a sense to justify the novel's title. The novel
begins:

> Dusk—of a summer night.
> And the tall walls of the commercial heart of an
> American city of perhaps 400,000 inhabitants—such
> walls as in time may linger as a mere fable.
> And up the broad street, now comparatively hushed,
> a little band of six,—a man of about fifty, short, stout,
> with bushy hair protruding from under a round black
> felt hat, a most unimportant-looking person, who car-
> ried a small portable organ such as is customarily used
> by street preachers and singers. And with him a woman
> perhaps five years his junior, taller, not so broad, but
> solid of frame and vigorous, very plain in face and
> dress, and yet not homely, leading with one hand a
> small boy of seven and in the other carrying a Bible and
> several hymn books. With these three, but walking inde-
> pendently behind, was a girl of fifteen, a boy of twelve
> and another girl of nine, all following obediently; but
> not too enthusiastically, in the wake of the others.
> It was hot, yet with a sweet languor about it all. [15]

And towards the end of the novel:

> Dusk, of a summer night.
> And the tall walls of the commercial heart of the city
> of San Francisco—tall and gray in the evening shade.
> And up a broad street from the south of Market—now
> comparatively hushed after the din of the day, a little
> band of five—a man of about sixty, short, stout, yet
> cadaverous as to the flesh of his face—and more espe-
> cially about the pale, dim eyes—and with bushy white
> hair protruding from under a worn, round felt hat—a
> most unimportant and exhausted looking person, who
> carried a small, portable organ such as is customarily
> used by street preachers and singers. And by his side, a
> woman not more than five years his junior—taller, not so

broad, but solid of frame and vigorous—with snow white hair and wearing an unrelieved costume of black—dress, bonnet, shoes. And her face broader and more characterful than her husband's, but more definitely seamed with lines of misery and suffering. At her side, again, carrying a Bible and several hymn books—a boy of not more than seven or eight—very round-eyed and alert, who, because of some sympathetic understanding between him and his elderly companion, seemed to desire to walk close to her—a brisk and smart stepping—although none-too-well dressed boy. . . .

It was hot, with the sweet languor of a Pacific summer about it all. [871–72]

Book I ends with Clyde involved in a car accident that forces him to leave Kansas City. He is fleeing the police:

Clyde . . . began crawling upon his hands and knees at first in the snow south, south and west, always toward some of those distant streets which, lamplit and faintly glowing, he saw to the southwest of him, and among which presently, if he were not captured, he hoped to hide—to lose himself and so escape—if the fates were only kind—the misery and the punishment and the unending dissatisfaction and disappointment which now, most definitely, it all represented to him. [161]

Book II opens with a description of the lavish home of Clyde's uncle, Samuel Griffiths, presenting at once a sharp contrast with the shoddy surroundings Clyde knew in Kansas City. It also presents a promise, a possibility for Clyde to move from poverty to wealth.

The home of Samuel Griffiths in Lycurgus, New York, a city of some twenty-five thousand inhabitants midway between Utica and New Albany. Near the dinner hour and by degrees the family assembling for its customary meal. On this occasion the preparations were of a more elaborate nature than usual, owing to the fact that for the past four days Mr. Samuel Griffiths, the husband and father, had been absent attending a conference of shirt and collar manufacturers in Chicago, price-cutting by upstart rivals in the west having necessitated compromise and adjustment by those who manufactured in the east. He was but now returned and had telephoned earlier in the afternoon that he had arrived, and was going to his office in the factory where he would remain until dinner time. [165]

Book II ends with the murder, and, just as in the end of Book I, Clyde is fleeing from a crime of which he may or may not be guilty. "And then the gloom, in spite of the summer stars. And a youth making his way through a dark, uninhabited wood, a dry straw hat upon his head, a bag in his hand, walking briskly yet warily—south—south." [533] Book III begins with a description of the county where Clyde is to be placed on trial, and it ends as Clyde leaves his life and as his nephew starts out on his.

There are many uses of deliberately plotted ironies. When Clyde's unmarried sister becomes pregnant, Clyde thinks about the traveling actor who seduced her.

But what a dog that man was to go off and leave his sister in a big strange city without a dime. He puzzled, thinking now of the girl who had been in the Green-Davidson some months before with a room and board unpaid. And how comic it had seemed to him and the other boys at the time—highly colored with a sensual interest in it.

But this, well, this was his own sister. A man had thought so little of his sister as that. And yet, try as he would, he could no longer think that it was as terrible as when he heard her crying in the room. Here was this brisk, bright city about him running with people and effort, and this gay hotel in which he worked. That was not so bad. Besides there was his own love affair, Hortense, and pleasures. [112–13]

Later, of course, Clyde himself assumes the role of the violator, not merely leaving the girl he seduces, but plotting to kill her as well.

Clyde's later involvement with Sondra Finchley, with her beauty and wealth, is foreshadowed by an earlier flirtation in Kansas City with a cheap, grasping girl who has expensive tastes. " 'An' your eyes are just like soft, black velvet,' he persisted eagerly. 'They're wonderful.' He was thinking of an alcove in the Green-Davidson hung with black velvet." [125] For Clyde, sex and wealth form a fatal attraction, leading directly to the automobile crash as well as to Roberta's death.

The novel pivots about the murder scene. To quote John Berryman, "the center of it is the murder (legal and moral up to a point, and then only moral)." [9] Clyde's first social meeting with Roberta takes place while he is in a boat, the crime takes place in a boat. Returning to Sondra and her society friends, Clyde once more finds himself on a lake, this time a speedboat: "And Burchard, throwing the boat from side to side as swiftly as he dared, with Jill Trumbull, anxious for her own safety, calling: 'Oh, say, what do you want to do. Drown us all?' " [581]

Clyde is taught to dance, early in the book, and this is his first mastery of the social graces which enable him to rise to the top of Lycurgus society. Later, he teaches Roberta to dance. Sondra, in turn, teaches Clyde a number of useful things. When Clyde becomes involved with Sondra, and wishes to forget Roberta, the two girls, one socially inferior to Clyde, the other his better, are juxtaposed. Roberta is about to leave the factory due to her advanced pregnancy at the same time Sondra is about to leave the city for her parents' summer home on the lake. Sondra is to Clyde as Clyde is to Roberta. Roberta wants to marry Clyde; Clyde in turn wants Sondra to elope with him. Either move would do great harm to the social position of the superior and advance the social status of the other.

Roberta and Clyde have similar backgrounds, separated only by Clyde's assumption that he can force his dreams into reality with the assistance of his rich relatives. Roberta's rural background is a rustic version of Clyde's city childhood. Her father, a nebulous failure, like Clyde's, "was a farmer solely because his father had been a farmer." He handed his beliefs down to Roberta, just as Clyde's father did to his son, and like Clyde, Roberta was capable of dreaming of a more thrilling life: "So it was that although throughout her infancy and girlhood she was compelled to hear of and share a depriving and toilsome poverty, still, because of her innate imagination, she was always thinking of something better. Maybe, some day, who knew, a larger city like Albany or Utica! A newer and greater life." [269] Even Clyde, while contemplating murdering Roberta, could, "for some reason almost see himself in Roberta's place." Roberta is Clyde without the lucky breaks, and in killing her Clyde is cutting himself off from his past and from his reality.

An amusing if not devastating irony is found in Clyde's anxious attitude as he nears social prominence. He snubs new found friends. "What! Mix with people so far below him—a Griffiths—in the social scale here and at the cost of endangering his connection with that important family. Never! It was a great mistake." [235] He is never on safe ground; afraid of his past and unsure of his future role he divorces himself from all possible help on his own level. The rich world he tries to enter will never completely accept him, yet Clyde is so taken by the desire to be a part of it that even at his arrest he begs not to be handcuffed in sight of the playboys and playgirls.

When Clyde first bumbles into Lycurgus society he is invited to a party and is awkwardly miserable, staring in envy at the assured and casual members of the group. When he is arrested, we find him an active member of this same group he was once in awe of, able to chatter about trivialities. The moment he arrives at his goal is the very moment at which everything he has plotted for is threatened.

The final irony does not involve Clyde; it is concerned with Russell, the illegitimate son of Clyde's sister, "a dark-haired child, in some ways resembling Clyde, who, even at this early age, as Clyde had been before him, was being instructed in those fundamental verities which had irritated Clyde in his own childhood." [670] For though Russell, like Clyde, is introduced to us on a beautiful summer's day, he too may very well be brought to trial on "another miserable, black and weary night. And then another miserable gray and wintry morning." [715]

iv

More than any of Dreiser's other novels, *An American Tragedy* is about America, and throughout the book we have the steady theme of why, for Clyde and many others, it is a tragic America. According to Matthiessen, "Dreiser's central thought in putting the word American into his title was the overwhelming lure of money-values in our society, more nakedly apparent than in older and more complex social structures. And just as the flame was more bright and compelling, so were its victims drawn to it more helplessly." [10]

We know that Dreiser carefully studied various criminal cases before he decided on one that embodied the problems he was most interested in fictionalizing. He chose a 1906 case in which Chester Gillette was convicted of murdering Grace Brown, only after going over fifteen other murders. Mrs. Dreiser has written of Dreiser's final choice:

> Theodore had already described to me how and why he had finally chosen the Chester Gillette–Grace Brown case for the framework of his story, after pondering for many years over various cases which presented the psychological problem he was most interested in. This problem had been forced on his mind not only by the extreme American enthusiasm for wealth as contrasted with American poverty, but the determination of so many young Americans, boys and girls alike, to obtain wealth quickly by marriage. When he realized the nature of the American literature of that period and what was being offered and consumed by publishers and public, he also became aware of the fact that the most interesting American story of the day concerned not only the boy getting the girl, but more emphatically, the poor boy getting the rich girl. Also, he came to know that it was a natural outgrowth of the crude pioneering conditions of American life up to that time, based on the glorification of wealth which started with the early days of slavery and persisted throughout our history.[11]

Chester Gillette was executed on March 31, 1908, after New York Governor Charles Evans Hughes refused Mrs. Gillette's pleas to spare her boy. The afternoon before the execution Gillette made a full confession. According to Hughes, "That night, I went to bed and slept soundly. It was my first refreshing sleep for a long time." Gillette, who had spent two years at Oberlin College, was working in a shirt factory in upstate New York where he met Grace Brown, a twenty-year-old farm girl. They became lovers, and when she was four months pregnant, Gillette took her on a fatal boatride on Big Moose Lake in the Adirondacks,

"hired a boat, rowed to a secluded spot, and there, the
state said, beat her savagely and threw her into the
water. Gillette claimed she had jumped in after he told
her he would not marry her." Gillette is buried in an
unmarked prison grave which faces east, according to
his mother's wishes, so he "shall lie where the sun each
day shall rest first on his grave . . . you know Chester's sunny disposition." [12]

Dreiser altered some basic aspects of the Gillette
case. He stressed the accidental aspect of the murder
(Gillette struck Grace Brown deliberately, using a tennis racket). Dreiser had Roberta struck by a camera
and hit by part of the rowboat as she fell. Clyde's guilt
is not in striking a deliberate blow, but in failing to
swim to the rescue. The camera, however, serves as
well as a tennis racket to symbolize the type of life
Clyde wanted.

Dreiser's interest, of course, was more in the America which helped form Chester, than in the crime itself. His first plan was to entitle the novel *Mirage*, and
it was this aspect of the case that obviously intrigued
him.

Since the beginning of his days as a newspaperman, he
had been aware of a certain type of crime seemingly
produced by financial and social aspiration, the murder
of some poorly placed girl by a young, ambitious lover
who was attempting to gain freedom to affiliate himself
with another girl more sophisticated and wealthy. The
young man was usually one who had first fallen in love
with someone of his own station, then had risen in the
world and met a second girl surpassing his original
sweetheart in glamour and affection, and finally, trying
to break old ties and encountering the complications of
the first girl's pregnancy, affection, and determination
to retain him, had in bewildered desperation committed
murder. Whether the hapless sweetheart was morally

right or practically foolish in her determination, Dreiser saw the situation as one which was produced by the very society that condemned the outcome.[13]

Dreiser agreed with Clarence Darrow's advice: "Listen to the story of anyone who has gone to prison, and see if he ever had a chance to go anywhere else." [14] In a book review Dreiser once stated that murderers would undoubtedly continue to ask forgiveness of God before going to the electric chair, but the novelist felt that it was Society that should ask forgiveness, "and perhaps God also." [15]

Dreiser chose well in using the Gillette case for his model. His study and deliberation was rewarded, for "he was sure that it was not only right for what he wanted to say, but also very typical of American life." As Clyde grows up we see his development in relation to many aspects of American life; in general the background shifts from lower to middle to upper class (the same pattern followed in *Sister Carrie* and *Jennie Gerhardt*), and Dreiser is certainly skillful in "pointing out the successive rungs of insecurity." [16] The picture is of the America Randolph Bourne saw as in the process of growing, and the interest Dreiser evokes "is part of that eager interest we feel in that growth." [17]

As a youngster, participating with his family in street services, Clyde was conscious of the stares of the passers-by "held by the peculiarity of such an unimportant-looking family publicly raising its collective voice against the vast skepticism and apathy of life." [16] Clyde was aware that his parents were different, more religious and certainly more isolated, and he felt ashamed. He felt left out of the excitement America had to offer. "The handsome automobiles that sped by, the loitering pedestrians moving off to what interests and comforts he could only surmise; the gay pairs of young people, laughing and jesting and the 'kids' staring, all troubled him with a sense of something different, better, more beautiful than his, or rather their life." [18]

Etta's pregnancy brings home the lesson that the outside world holds terror and danger as well as attraction, but Clyde is easily overcome by the same forces that ruin his sister's life. He scorned manual labor and all it implied, wearing old clothes, getting up early in the morning, and doing "all the commonplace things such people had to do." [26] Each job Clyde holds increases his desire to succeed; and each tells us more about America as Clyde works at many positions: in a drugstore, in two hotels and the Union League of Chicago, and finally in his uncle's collar factory.

The Green-Davidson Hotel presents the first concrete symbol of his American dream, and from his vantage point as bellboy, Clyde was both spectator and insider, "insanely eager for all the pleasures which he saw swirling around him." [61] The hotel was overly ornate:

> In short it was compact, of all that gauche luxury of appointment which, as some one once sarcastically remarked, was intended to supply "exclusiveness to the masses." Indeed, for an essential hotel in a great and successful American commercial city, it was almost too luxurious. Its rooms and halls and lobbies and restaurants were entirely too richly furnished, without the saving grace of either simplicity or necessity. [42]

The pleasures may be "imagined," but Clyde is eminently practical in his search for them, being able to take the measure of the other employees at the hotel, just as he later takes the measure of his co-workers at the collar factory. One interesting type Clyde studies and attempts to understand is epitomized in Mr.

Whiggam, a tense, forty year old minor functionary in the collar factory. "His head, as Clyde at once noticed, appeared chronically to incline forward, while at the same time he lifted his eyes as though actually he would prefer not to look up." [203] He is overawed in the presence of his superiors at the factory, but, when confronting those under his authority, he holds his head higher and speaks with assurance. He toadies to Clyde, knowing him to be related to the head of the concern. Whiggam obviously has calculated his position with a frightening precision; adapting himself to changeable roles of supervisor and employee, all the while constantly on the lookout to rise above his present position, to a higher one where the tensions would be all the greater.

Clyde, himself, gradually adopts a tone of condescension towards friends who will be of little use to him. At a church social he is pampered as the nephew of a rich man, though he does not quite succeed as he does not behave with sufficient insolence. The friend who clings to him shows him off to the gathering, whispering such remarks as "She don't amount to anything. Her father only keeps a small garage here. I wouldn't bother with her if I were you." [224]

But the lesson that most impresses Clyde is not the way the middle class will debase itself; he learns of the appalling gap between economic groups in America. He watches a parade in Lycurgus, replete with floats on which are perched the rich, beautiful and happy society girls he dreams of. He is a spectator, and a lonely one at that, hovering between the two worlds, denied one and unhappy with the other, discovering, as Roberta had, that "the lines of demarcation and stratification between the rich and the poor in Lycurgus were as sharp as though cut by a knife or divided by a high wall." [274–75] Clyde is warned against associating with the help, yet socially he is far from accepted by his uncle's crowd.

High society is a revelation to Clyde. It is a limited world "where quite every one who has anything at all knew every one, the state of one's purse was as much, and in some instances even more, considered than one's social connections. For these local families of distinction were convinced that not only one's family but one's wealth was the be-all and end-all of every happy union meant to include social security." [394] But only after the murder do we see how these supposedly socially secure families are capable of the same fears as lesser members of the Lycurgus community. Clyde's aunt and uncle are more concerned with their loss of status than with the crime or Clyde. Thus, Dreiser's picture of the social classes in America is complete as we learn that Clyde is far from being alone in his ambition to rise. His unsureness, his fear of social disapproval, his compensating need to look down on those less successful, is all part of the America he is a part of. And when he does achieve fame of a sort, when his trial makes newspaper headlines, Clyde becomes a symbol of the American dream gone wrong, for, in essence, his story is an essential part of America.

v

The failure of religion to cope with the problems of American life was the central thesis of *The Bulwark*, and religion played a minor, climactic part in the Cowperwood trilogy and *The "Genius."* In *An American Tragedy* religion is studied in relation to Clyde and his growth, and two attitudes of religion towards America are shown: the fundamental, uncompromising religion and the religion that plays along with the American dream. Each of the three books of the novel brings up religion, and religion is shown, in all cases, as failing Clyde; and the implication of the final street scenes, echoing the opening scenes, is that it will continue to fail Clyde's nephew and America as well.

Clyde is exposed to two exponents of raw, Messianic religion—in early childhood and, again, just before his death. His mother's narrow, bed-rock religious philosophy is repeatedly shown as well-meaning, impractical, and often harmful. She never understands her son or the forces tempting him. Hearing of Clyde's trial she wrings her "large, rough hands" and prays in a room plastered with signs which proclaim "the charity, the wisdom, and the sustaining righteousness of God." [673] She retains her faith despite her many hardships. When Clyde's sister was seduced, Mrs. Griffiths had momentary doubts, but these doubts are only momentary for, "in some blind, dualistic way both she and Asa insisted . . . in disassociating God from harm and error and misery, while granting Him nevertheless supreme control." [32] Clyde, however, never accepts his mother's beliefs. "Mission work was nothing. All this religious emotion and talk was not so much either. It hadn't saved Etta. Evidently, like himself, she didn't believe so much in it, either." [35]

Clyde's mother, absent as an influence during the time he is away from home, re-enters her son's life after the murder.

> And now this American witness to the rule of God upon earth, sitting in a chair in her shabby, nondescript apartment, hard-pressed for the very means to sustain herself —degraded by the milling forces of life and the fell and brutal blows of chance—yet serene in her trust—and declaring: I cannot think this morning, I seem numb and things look strange to me. My boy found guilty of murder! But I am his mother and I am not convinced of his guilt by any means! He has written me that he is not

guilty and I believe him. And to whom should he turn
with the truth and for trust if not to me? But there is He
who sees all things and who knows. [798]

Clyde is visited in prison by Reverend Duncan Mc-
Millan, who echoes his mother's fervor and succeeds,
to a degree, in reaching the boy. He reads aloud
Psalm 51, and Clyde listens with astonishment. But
McMillan has come too late.

An American Tragedy shows us more than the
religious fanatic. The Babbitry of watered Christianity
is presented, and in one case is balanced against Mrs.
Griffiths' religion. Mrs. Griffiths attempts to raise
money to save Clyde, but the local ministers are not
moved to any action and are scornful of this lady
who "in defiance of all the tenets and processes of organized and historic . . . religious powers and forms,"
chooses "to walk forth and without ordination after
any fashion conduct an unauthorized and hence non-
descript mission. Besides if she had remained at
home, as a good mother should, and devoted herself to
her son, as well as to her other children—their care
and education—would this—have happened?" [822]

Clyde, shortly after arriving in Lycurgus, is introduced to a typical church scene, a "semi-religious,
semi-social and semi-emotional" [222–23] affair. The
elders gossip, the younger members flirt, and religion
seems to have been forgotten. When Clyde is in trouble he consults a druggist who would not "trifle"
against the laws of God, yet "at the same time he was
too good a merchant to alienate a possible future customer" and suggests Clyde try some other shops. "His
manner as he spoke was solemn, the convinced and
earnest tone and look of the moralist who knows that
he is right." [411] American religion is shown as shal-
low and opportunistic. Clyde's lawyer gives his client
some sound advice when he tells him to attend the

Sunday jail services, "For this is a religious community, and I want you to make as good an impression
as you can." [65]

The failure of American religion comes to sharp
focus during Clyde's imprisonment. One of his fellow
prisoners in the death-house is a religious maniac,
crawling on the floor and licking the feet of a brass
Christ on a cross. Clyde, facing death, wonders about
religion, but considers the fruitless prayers of his
family. "Was he going to turn to religion now, solely
because he was in difficulties and frightened like
these others?" [840] Saying farewell to his mother, he
still doubts. " 'Mama, you must believe that I die re-
signed and content. It won't be hard. God had heard
my prayers. He has given me strength and peace.' But
to himself adding: 'Had he?' " [869]

Clyde, during his brief lifetime, was thus exposed
to two aspects of American religious life. The faith of
his mother and Reverend McMillan was blind to the
attractions of America; and the religion which tried to
accept America and conform to its demands became
ridiculous. Part of the American tragedy, as viewed by
Dreiser and presented through the story of Clyde
Griffiths, was the failure of religion to be a responsible
force for good.

In *Jennie Gerhardt* Dreiser studied two families at
opposite ends of America's social scale and showed
how both were adversely affected by the new American
values. Dreiser uses the identical technique in *An
American Tragedy*, contrasting Clyde's family with
the rich household of Samuel Griffiths. In both families
the children are in rebellion; in the poor family the
children escape, one to return home in disgrace, the
other never to come back; in the rich family the children turn into class-conscious hypocrites, lacking both
the strength and the sense of their parents.

Clyde's parents, like Jennie's, were religious extremists, and the boy never regarded himself as part of their world. He was able to study the family situation with a frightening objectivity, "not too sharply or bitterly, but with a very fair grasp of their qualities and capabilities." [27] Clyde saw that the outside world, with all its tantalizing joys, could only be reached if he rejected his parents. "He began to sense the delight of personal freedom—to sniff the air of personal and delicious romance—and he was not to be held back by any suggestion which his mother could now make." [67]

In jail, awaiting death, Clyde is reunited with his mother. "Whatever her faults or defects, after all she was his mother, wasn't she?" [807] Clyde thinks back on his childhood, recalling the dreary mission life and his resentment at being different. His mother never understood. "It was as though there was an insurmountable wall . . . built by the lack of understanding. . . . She would never understand his craving for ease and luxury, for beauty, for love—his particular kind of love that went with show, pleasure, wealth, position, his eager and immutable aspirations and desires. She could not understand these things." [866] And she never understood, for the novel ends as she leads Clyde's nephew through the yellow door of a mission house.

Samuel Griffiths, capable and successful, serves as the obvious contrast to Clyde's father, but like his brother he fails to develop a meaningful relationship with his children. Even Clyde is aware of the "tone of condescension" [241] which Gilbert uses with his father. Gilbert, like most of Dreiser's characters who inherit rather than earn their wealth, is shown to be as pompous as he is weak, chatting about "the social importance of the collar business" which gives "polish and manner to people who wouldn't otherwise have them." [352] When Clyde's crime is revealed Samuel, at least, tries to understand. He blames himself for contributing to Clyde's unhappiness. Even Gil is forced to reflect on his father's fairness. "His father was a man, really. He might be cruelly wounded and distressed, but, unlike himself, he was neither petty nor revengeful." [634] The "great social gap between them" [667–68] prevents a meeting between Clyde's parents and his aunt and uncle, and it is only in relation to Clyde that the two families can be juxtaposed. Neither family is able to help the boy, just as neither family functions as an effective unit.

Though Dreiser, in most of his novels, unfortunately rumbles on about "chemic compulsions" between his characters, and though, in *The "Genius"* he makes a woeful attempt at equating artistic failure with sexual indulgence, in *An American Tragedy* he does manage to refrain from moralizing. As a result we have sex presented as part of his story of Clyde Griffiths and America, part of the dream gone wrong, something beautiful robbed of its potential goodness. Clyde, from the first, never accepts sex as anything but a reflection of ambition. Breaking away from his religious home for the first time, he works in a drugstore (which like the hotel is set up as the ornate symbol of temptation) and stares at the girls who come to the counter. Clyde, "callow and inexperienced in the ways of the world, and those of the opposite sex, was never weary of observing the beauty, the daring, the self-sufficiency and the sweetness of these as he saw them. . . . The wonder of them!" [37–38]

Sex is thus early equated with the American dream, and Clyde, being as eagerly susceptible as his sister, is easily made a victim of both. His first real affair, with Hortense Briggs, sets the pattern. He is used. Sex becomes, not part of a meaningful relationship, but something to acquire, as partial reward for having achieved a goal. Sex is material, the result of buying gifts and flattering; and as Clyde moves up the social ladder, his sexual adventures reflect his progress. One of his tragedies is that he is unable to establish a firm relationship with any woman. Sondra, his great love, for whom he even contemplates murder, arouses "a curiously stinging sense of what it was to want and not to have." [242–43] During the trial Clyde's attitude towards Sondra never changes. He is horrified by the suggestion that, although he seduced and killed Roberta, he might also have seduced Sondra. This would have been an insult, Sondra would never have allowed such liberties, and "you don't want to forget who she is." [647] She is, of course, not a person but the personification of the upper class.

Sex becomes a curious part of the American dream, not a driving force of love but a symbol of achievement. Like American religion it has been cheapened, and one reason for the success of *An American Tragedy* is Dreiser's ability, for the first time in any of his novels, to make sex part of his characters and part of his story and not some mysterious force that hovers above both. The argument that Dreiser fails as a writer because he supposedly claims a rigid determinism is belied by his novels. We suffer along with his characters; for we know, as they do, the nature of their handicaps and limitations, and the very act of *trying* to improve rules out a hundred per cent, superimposed, mechanical universe.

vi

Dreiser did more than bring together various aspects of American life in his novels; he created characters capable of demonstrating his theses. His books are important, then, not simply as sociological studies but because he pictures the economic and social forces in operation on believable people for whom we care. In *An American Tragedy* we have Roberta Alden and Clyde Griffiths.

Woman, as Joseph Warren Beach has pointed out, gets the worst of it in Dreiser's novels; "condemned to checkmate in the ruthless game of hearts . . . with her disposition to loyalty, her absolute adherence to the conventional standards governing the married state, her relative weakness economically and biologically." [18]

One of the self-styled "humanistic" critics of Dreiser, Robert Shafer, sees Roberta merely as "the inevitable resultant of inheritance, environment, and sex," and feels she never emerges as a person but only as "an embodied energy," having "the same significance as the squirming of an angleworm, impaled by some mischievous boy—no less, but certainly no more." [19] It is true that Dreiser goes into Roberta's farm background soon after she is introduced, but we already are sympathetic towards this tense and pretty girl, obviously a dreamer, who tries so hard to get along with her fellow workers. And the several pages devoted to her unfortunate childhood do not make her an "embodied energy" but point up her courage and decency.

> The reasons why a girl of Roberta's type should be seeking employment with Griffiths and Company at this time and in this capacity are of some point. For somewhat after the fashion of Clyde in relation to his family and his life, she too considered her life a great disappointment. She was the daughter of Titus Alden, a farmer—of near Biltz, a small town in Mimico County, some fifty miles north. And her youth up she had seen little but poverty. Her father—the youngest of three sons . . . was so unsuccessful that at forty-eight he was

still living in a house which, though old and much in need of repair at the time his father willed it to him, was now bordering upon a state of dilapidation. The house itself, while primarily a charming example of that excellent taste which produced those delightful gabled homes which embellish the average New England town and street, had been by now so reduced for want of paint, shingles, . . . that it presented a rather melancholy aspect to the world. [268]

Roberta, moving to Lycurgus, rooms with a home-town friend, an unhappy, emotionally starved girl who demands to share an active part in Roberta's life and is inevitably rebuffed as Roberta falls in love with Clyde. Roberta moves to a single room, and from then on her character is shown in terms of her love for Clyde and her fear of being betrayed. She is aware of her difficult position, and part of her tragedy is implicit in this awareness. Being aware, she suffers, and being aware this suffering has a significance which the critics of Dreiser seldom understand. Here are three paragraphs, from three different chapters, which illustrate the point.

Nevertheless, her underlying thought in connection with all this, in so far as Clyde and his great passion for her was concerned—and hers for him—was that she was indeed trifling with fire and perhaps social disgrace into the bargain. For, although consciously at this time she was scarcely willing to face the fact that this room—its geometric position in relation to the rest of the house—had been of the greatest import to her at the time she first saw it, yet subconsciously she knew it well enough. The course she was pursuing was dangerous—that she knew. And yet how, as she now so often asked herself at moments when she was confronted by some desire which ran counter to her sense of practicability and social morality, was she to do? [314]

The state of Roberta's mind for that night is not easily to be described. For here was true and poignant love, and in youth true and poignant love is difficult to withstand. Besides it was coupled with the most grandiose illusions in regard to Clyde's local material and social condition—illusions which had little to do with anything he had done to build up, but were based on conjecture and gossip over which he had no control. And her own home, as well as her personal situation, was so unfortunate—no promise of any kind save in his direction. And here she was quarreling with him—sending him away angry. On the other hand was he not beginning to push too ardently toward those troublesome and no doubt dreadful liberties and familiarities which her morally trained conscience would not permit her to look upon as right? How was she to do now? What to say? [321]

Two incidents which occurred at this time tended still more to sharpen the contrary points of view holding between Clyde and Roberta. One of these was no more than a glimpse which Roberta had one evening of Clyde pausing at the Central Avenue curb in front of the post-office to say a few words to Arabella Stark, who in a large and impressive-looking car, was waiting for her father, who was still in the Stark Building opposite. And Miss Stark, fashionably outfitted according to the season, her world and her own pretentious taste, was affectedly posed at the wheel, not only for the benefit of Clyde but the public in general. And to Roberta, who by now was reduced to the verge of distraction between Clyde's delay and her determination to compel him to act in her behalf, she appeared to be little less than an epitome of all the security, luxury, and freedom from responsibility which so enticed and hence caused Clyde to delay and be as indifferent as possible to the dire state which confronted her. For, alas, apart from this claim of her condition, what had she to offer him comparable to all he would be giving up in case he acceded to her request?

Nothing—a thought which was far from encouraging. [461–62]

Roberta, mourned by her father as a "good, kind, faithful daughter," is a girl whose hope and decency ends in failure. That her failure is, in a large part, due to the pressures of society does not make her an automaton, nor does it make her struggle less real or less tragic.

Though *An American Tragedy* is far from being a one-character book (in the sense that the Cowperwood trilogy is) it is Dreiser's success in creating a believable Clyde Griffiths that makes the novel important. We care what happens to Clyde for we understand him: sensitive, selfish, and above all, weak, he has what John Chamberlain correctly terms "symbolic truth" as well as an obvious authenticity. "Clyde Griffiths may not represent America in its better moments, but he represents one American aspiration, at any rate." [20]

It is these seemingly contradictory elements in Clyde—the sensitivity, the selfishness, the weakness —that run through his story, and it is the sensitivity that sets the tragedy in motion. Far from being a "genius," Clyde nevertheless does resemble Eugene Witla in his painful awareness of a potentially more exciting life. Dreiser stresses Clyde's sensitivity. Even as a child he was "much too responsive to phases of beauty and pleasure which had little, if anything, to do with the remote and cloudy romance which swayed the minds of his mother and father." [17] At fifteen he regarded his life as "shabby," his parents as "ineffectual." [22, 25] Breaking from the family discipline, working in the hotel, "the world had changed for him entirely." [52] Later, working in Lycurgus, he makes love to Roberta: "He looked up and before him in the east over the low roofs of the city was the thinnest, yellowest topmost arc of the rising July moon. It seemed at the moment as though life had given him all—all—that he could possibly ask of it." [301] And when he rejects Roberta, he could "for some reason almost see himself in Roberta's place." [392] This sensitivity comes to focus in the effective prison scenes in Book III.

> And Clyde thereafter—lonely—terribly so. Now there was no one here—no one—in whom he was interested. He could only sit and read—and think—or pretend to be interested in what these others said, for he could not really be interested in what they said. His was a mind that, freed from the miseries that had now befallen him, was naturally more drawn to romance than to reality. Where he read at all he preferred the light, romantic novel that pictured some such world as he would have liked to share, to anything that even approximated the hard reality of the world, let alone this. Now what was to become of him eventually? [833–34]

Facing death, Clyde contemplates his life, feeling that his judgers do not understand him, for "they had not burned with that unquenchable passion for the Sondra of his beautiful dream." [857] He faces death courageously, remembering "the few, brief, intense moments. His desire for more." [864]

Clyde's sensitivity, however, is to a large extent overshadowed by his vanity, his actively demonstrated selfishness which is carefully documented by Dreiser. "For Clyde was as vain and proud as he was poor. He was one of those interesting individuals who looked upon himself as a thing apart—never quite wholly and indissolubly merged with the family of which he was a member, and never with any profound obligations to those who had been responsible for his coming into the world." [27]

Working as a bellboy at the Hotel Green-Davidson, Clyde lies to his parents about his salary and hours and spends the money, obviously needed by his family, on flashy clothes. Hearing of his sister's trouble, he feels, not pity, but "a little sick and resentful." [109] After the automobile crash (following a joy ride in a stolen car) he thinks, not of the other riders who might be injured, but only of himself. His flight from the city, just as his later flight from the lake, is a lonely, selfish decision. So it is not only a dreaming Clyde who comes to Lycurgus, but a sneaky opportunist as well. As previously noted, at the first realization of his social prominence he drops his early acquaintances. Meeting his cousin, Gilbert, he experiences envy as well as jealousy, and it is apparent that Clyde is simply a poorer version of the more fortunate relative. It is no surprise then that having made Roberta pregnant and having fallen in love with Sondra, Clyde is capable of plotting a murder. In one sense the prosecuting attorney is right when he refers to Clyde's mind as "a mature and not an immature one." [692]

But selfish and sensitive as he is, it is Clyde's fundamental weakness that we most understand, and F. O. Matthiessen is right in asserting that the main reason why Dreiser can make us feel touched by Clyde's feelings is that he is aware of how pathetic they really are. John Cowper Powys remarked of Dreiser that "no man I ever met is so sympathetic with weakness," [24] and certainly this capacity for sympathy is evident in the portrayal of Clyde.

The defense attorney, appealing to the jury, refers to his client as "a mental as well as a moral coward—no more and no less—not a downright criminal by any means." [721] Over and over this expression "mental and moral coward" is repeated during the trial scenes of Book III. And we come to realize how accurate this evaluation is, how the real tragedy of Clyde is that he is too weak, too unprepared to chase his dream. Dreiser, in Book II, described Clyde as having "a soul that was not destined to grow up." [189] His aunt, upon first meeting him, sizes him up as "soft and vague and fumbling." His cousin, Myra, sees him as resembling herself, "nervous and somewhat furtive and appealing or seeking." [238–39] Clyde is often characterized as confused and disturbed, as "having a temperament as fluid and unstable as water," [338] and usually as being intensely sorry for himself. "It was so hard to be poor, not to have money and position and to be able to do in life exactly as you wished." [292]

Facing and dodging the fact of Roberta's pregnancy, Clyde "was as interesting an illustration of the enormous handicaps imposed by ignorance, youth, poverty and fear as one could have found." [418] His fate was not inevitable, but it is explainable in terms of his sensitivity, his selfishness, and his weakness, a weakness which Dreiser ponders and explains, which is able to visualize the American dream but is unable to make it a reality. Clyde's, then, is the true American tragedy, and the novel about his life is Dreiser's best fictional expression of this tragedy.

vii

In this study I have tried to demonstrate that Dreiser's novels are carefully planned works of art, based on themes which have to do with problems inherent in American life. His books are thus more than idle slices of life; they are organized and meaningful studies, novels which are often both beautiful and powerful.

Sister Carrie, Dreiser's first novel, is in essence concerned with two key figures, Carrie and Hurstwood, whose tragic story dominates the work. In discussing this novel, Dreiser stated, "I never can and never want to bring myself to the place where I can ignore the sensitive and seeking individual in his pitiful struggle with nature—with his enormous urges and his pathetic equipment." For Dreiser "Life is a tragedy . . . the infinite suffering and deprivation of great masses of men and women upon whom existence has been thrust unasked appals me." [22] *Sister Carrie* is Dreiser's first lengthy presentation of the stories of individuals who faced this life.

Hurstwood is shown, at first, as a successful front-man for a popular, upper-class Chicago restaurant. We see him sacrifice a seemingly secure life for the love of Carrie Meeber, the wistful, naïve mistress of a flashy drummer. Hurstwood's slow descent to total failure is in contrast to Carrie's rise as an actress. By setting these two against one another, Dreiser shows us the effect of the American dream on two decent individuals. Only one other protagonist is carefully delineated in *Sister Carrie*. The career of Drouet, the ambitious salesman, remains relatively static, but he too suffers as life becomes a constant struggle for position. And, like Hurstwood, he too is fated to lose the lovely Carrie.

In *Jennie Gerhardt* we see not only the individual, but the American family almost destroyed by the American Dream. Instead of two individuals juxtaposed against one another, the burden of the story lies in the picture of two families, each a representative of opposite ends of the economic scale in our country. American poverty and American wealth are both portrayed and both fail to function effectively. Though the love story of Jennie and Lester is an important part of the novel, the two fathers, both failures in different ways, perhaps serve best to highlight the basic theme of the book. And the description of Papa Gerhardt's last days, so lovingly chronicled by Dreiser, contains some of his best writing.

In the Cowperwood trilogy (*The Financier, The Titan,* and *The Stoic*) Dreiser studies the effect of American life on that rare individual, the one almost prepared to struggle successfully. In most of his novels this strength is denied to his characters, for what they are given in its place is a tantalizing vision of a better life to aim for.

Frank Cowperwood, the hero of the trilogy of desire, achieves an almost godly success based on a tough, jungle philosophy set forth in the justly famous sequence where, as a child, he watches the battle between the lobster and the squid. Cowperwood applies all his energies to the complicated business world of a rapidly expanding America and becomes a master at controlling and exploiting public transportation lines. He becomes the archetype of the self-made American millionaire, and his story, with its public successes and personal torments, remains the best portrayal of this sensational American type we have yet had. Cowperwood, like the lobster, must always be in a battle and his life becomes a continual fight, without reason or rest.

Continuing his studies of different aspects of American life gone wrong, Dreiser attempted the difficult task of portraying the American artist. Being a writer and a student of music and art, Dreiser was close to his subject matter. The opening portions of *The "Genius"* are touching and perceptive. We see the growing pains, the excitement of the growing artist. Unfortunately, the novel as a whole is a failure, for in its later sections the fundamental action of the book, the study of forces harmful to the artist in America, is lost among meaningless pages of mysticism and confusion. The story of Eugene Witla, artist as well as commercial hack, is Dreiser's most uneven work.

Dreiser's most unusual novel is *The Bulwark*, the author's attempt to come to terms with the problem of religion in America. Dreiser deliberately chooses a Quaker for his hero, a man as honest and courageous as he is unperceptive. The theme which dominates this fine novel is reflected by all the characters and in all the events: how can religion, based on an antimaterialistic philosophy, come to terms with an American society which, in essence, is un-Christian? Solon's failure is seen as religion's failure; yet, at the conclusion of the book, some hope is held out for America, for Solon's defeat is a defeat with dignity.

Fortunately Dreiser's most ambitious novel is also his most successful. In *An American Tragedy* Dreiser uses all the themes he has employed in his other works, and the short life of Clyde Griffiths mirrors the hopes as well as the failures of the American dream. Many segments of American society are shown as Clyde moves from the poverty of his religiously obsessed parents to the wealth of fashionable society in a factory town. Clyde literally marches through America and his adventures, thrilling and tragic, become Dreiser's masterpiece.

Many of Dreiser's novels have obvious flaws, and the novelist is too often guilty of a peculiarly pompous prose style. This unfortunate trait is most in evidence on the occasions when Dreiser tries to interpret his stories in terms of fuzzy, philosophical generalities, when he refuses to allow the story to tell its own moral. His dialogue is especially weak when he tries to capture the speech patterns of the upper class. But despite these limitations his novels remain powerful studies of American life and American failure, and they are so because, for the most part, Dreiser does write well, and he does tune his characters and plots to whatever theme is at the heart of the novel.

6   THE SHORT STORIES
NO LIES IN THE DARKNESS

> *I see worthwhile books as truthful representations of life in some form—nothing more.*
>
> THEODORE DREISER
> *"Marriage—For One"*

STUDENTS USUALLY GET an unfortunate and inadequate introduction to Dreiser's fiction, for though his talent lies in the lengthier form of the novel, he too often is presented as a short-story writer. Assorted collegiate anthologies sandwich his contributions between the shorter efforts of Henry James and Ernest Hemingway, and it would, in truth, take a truly dedicated reader to be inspired to sample more of Dreiser's work.

Much of Dreiser's effects in his novels depends on a steady, cumulative emotive presentation, small, pointed, meaningful additions which add to the formal action of the fiction. The short stories too often read, not as complete architectonic units within themselves, but as compressed, dehydrated novels. In these cases the famed Dreiserian defects bulge out. Pompous, essentially show-off expressions are trotted out for no specific purpose. In "Free," for example, at an inappropriately dramatic moment we have the following: "It was a mirage. An ignis fatuus." [1] Superficial, sophomoric psychologizing is abundant.[2] "They were amazing, these variations in his own thoughts, almost chemic, not volitional, decidedly peculiar for a man who was supposed to know his own mind—only did one, ever?" [62] Worst of all are the stretches of clumsy, overwritten prose, much too typical of the magazine fiction of the time. A child dies, and "little Elwell had finally ceased to be as flesh and was eventually carried forth to the lorn, disagreeable graveyard near Woodlawn." As for the father: "How he had groaned internally, indulged in sad, despondent thoughts concerning the futility of all things human, when this had happened!" [52] And these lapses, lamentable in Dreiser's realistic tales, become absurd in his feeble efforts at fantasy (such as in "McEwen of the Shining Slave Makers," "Khat," and "The Prince Who Was a Thief").

Though a few of the stories are of interest (especially two of the three we will look at—"Nigger Jeff," and "The Lost Phoebe") there is little to support James T. Farrell's contention that they rank among the best written in America during this century[3] or Howard Fast's belief that Dreiser has "no peer in the American story."[4] It is interesting that Sherwood Anderson, who wrote the introduction to a 1918 edition of Dreiser's stories, never becomes specific with his judgments. His tribute is a general one, in praise of a man "who with the passage of time is bound to loom larger and larger in the awakening consciousness of America," who is brave, and who was no trickster. Most important of all, he sees Dreiser the hero of an American movement aiming "toward courage and fidelity to life in writing," and notes that "the beauty and the ironic terror of life is like a wall before him but he faces the wall."[5] Certainly Dreiser is, as always, sincere and honest, boy scout virtues which are not, in themselves, enough for a writer. Only in a very few controlled, shorter works did he manage to approach the strength of his better novels.

Howard Fast was right in commenting that Dreiser "painted not with the quick, nervous brush of today, but in large planes and solid masses." This slabbish quality is probably best seen in "Free," a flashback tale which depressingly plunges us into the study of a seemingly successful architect whose wife is dying and who realizes, to his horror, that life, for him, was but a series of pitiful compromises. "Like the Spartan boy, he had concealed the fox gnawing at his vitals. He had not complained." [45] Now he complains, and with a vengeance.

A longer story than most of Dreiser's, "Free" has a structural unity, an action based on the wife as the symbol for the architect's essential lack of nerve.

> But even that was not the worst. No; that was not the worst, either. It had been the gradual realization coming along through the years that he had married an essentially small, narrow woman who could never really grasp his point of view—or, rather, the significance of his dreams or emotions—and yet with whom, nevertheless, because of this original promise or mistake, he was compelled to live. Grant her every quality of goodness, energy, industry, intent—as he did freely—still there was this; and it could never be adjusted, never. Essentially, as he had long since discovered, she was narrow, ultra-conventional, whereas he was an artist by nature, brooding and dreaming strange dreams and thinking of far-off things which she did not or could not understand or did not sympathize with, save in a general and very remote way. The nuances of his craft, the wonders and subtleties of forms and angles—had she ever realized how significant these were to him, let alone to herself? No, never. She had not the least true appreciation of them—never had had. Architecture? Art? What could

they really mean to her, desire as she might to appreciate them? And he could not now go elsewhere to discover that sympathy. No. He had never really wanted to, since the public and she would object, and he thinking it half evil himself. [46–47]

Rufus Haymaker (other names in the narrative include Elwell, Ethelberta, and Ottilie) is vague in his anger, never really focusing on specific targets and less intense than the middle-aged heroes of, say, Sherwood Anderson, Thomas Wolfe, or William Faulkner. It is a formless rage aimed, not at his wife, his spoiled children, or even American society, but at heavy, Dreiserian fate. "Cruel Nature, that cared so little for the dreams of man—the individual man or woman." [47] If ever there was a tale nakedly revealing the naturalistic movement's effect on the American writer, this is it. "Almost like a bird in a cage, an animal peeping out from behind bars, he had viewed the world of free thought and freer action." [49]

Perhaps the ruminations and outbursts of Haymaker have relevance to Dreiser's own peculiar marital troubles; in any case they do betray some of the blatantly adolescent attitudes about sex which marred *The "Genius."* "Think of it! He to whom so many women had turned with questioning eyes!" [48]

After a long chronicle of repressions and chances missed, Haymaker looks into a mirror. The theme of the story is recapitulated. "The figure he made here as against his dreams of a happier life, once he were free, now struck him forcibly. What a farce! What a failure!" [68] And summarizing it all, the meaning of his failure, he wonders just what he had missed. With his wife's death he will be free; but it is too late. He is free only to die. What has happened here is that a novel is compressed into shorter form. We never understand even a small part of Haymaker, his life or his development; in consequence his problem, stated over and over, is essentially meaningless as it doesn't involve a defined character. Dreiser misuses the short-story form here, and "Free" unfortunately becomes a parody of his poorer novels.

While "free" is an artistic failure, "Nigger Jeff," which at first seems just one more protest tale of a lynch mob and its victim, develops into a well-structured, meaningful story centered on the reactions of a bewildered young city reporter who faces organized violence for the first time. The action lies in our discovery of how Elmer Davies reacts to the horrifying event and what he discovers about America and himself.

Davies is introduced as "a vain and rather self-sufficient youth who was inclined to be of that turn of mind which sees in life only a fixed and ordered process of rewards and punishments." [157] At first he believes in the justice of the forthcoming lynching and is concerned only with the story he must write. Arriving at Pleasant Valley he notices the white houses "and the shimmering beauty of the small stream one had to cross in going from the depot." [159] Throughout the narrative Dreiser, as Crane before him, will inject descriptions of the placid countryside, almost as direct counterpoint to the frightening events taking place. As the mob hurries on, "the night was so beautiful that it was all but poignant . . . and the east promised a golden moon." [166] Again: "Slowly the silent company now took its way up the Sand River Pike whence it had come. The moon was still high, pouring down a wash of silvery light." [176] At the lynching "the pale light over the glimmering water seemed human and alive." [177] And as Davies sits, watching the dangling form, "the light of morning broke, a tender lavender and gray in the east. . . . Still the body hung there black and limp against the sky, and now a light breeze sprang up and stirred it visibly." [178] Finally, after the body is cut down, it is placed in a small cabin and Davies watches the rapist's mother weeping over her son Jeff. "All the corners of the room were quite dark. Only its middle was brightened by splotches of silvery light." [181]

Along with balancing the transcending wonders of nature with the human agonies, Dreiser also details Davies' petty dealings which are necessary to his reporting assignment. He is forced to haggle and connive. These three elements: the powerful landscape, the tragedy played out in front of it, and the reporter's small movements have their effects on Davies. His attitude towards life is different. "The knowledge now that it was not always exact justice that was meted out to all and that it was not so much the business of the writer to indict as to interpret was borne in on him with distinctness by the cruel sorrow of the mother, whose blame, if any, was infinitesimal." [182]

Robert Elias feels that in his stories Dreiser restates "his belief that nature must prevail . . . the subject of each story served to show that individuals were limited by circumstances or feelings for which only an inscrutable and indifferent nature appeared to be responsible. Men and women, created in one image, could not make themselves over in any other, and if there was a solution to their predicaments, no one knew it." [6] Perhaps. But man can learn. "Nigger Jeff" ends with the reporter's crying out his new ambition, as a man and as a writer. "I'll get it all in!" [182] In no sense does Jeff become a Joe Christmas, for Dreiser, unlike Faulkner, did not write a complicated allegory of modern man's betrayal. He simply told of one man's discovery; and this tale, carefully constructed, is a strong and moving work.

Dreiser's strangest story, "The Lost Phoebe," had a curious publishing history. Though completed in 1912, four years elapsed before it was finally accepted for publication. Even Dreiser's champions were shocked by the tale. In a letter to Dreiser, H. L. Mencken noted: "Nathan is so full of the notion that this 'Lost Phoebe' lies far off of the Dreiser that we want to play up that I begin to agree with him." [7]

"The Lost Phoebe" relates the pathetic wanderings of an aged, lonely farmer who is unable to accept the reality of his wife's death. For seven years he stumbles around the countryside, kept up by "spiritual endurance." Finally, one night, he believes he truly sees his late wife, younger, more beautiful. "He had been expecting and dreaming of this hour all these years, and now as he saw the feeble light dancing lightly before him he peered at it questioningly, one thin hand in his gray hair." Old Henry Reifsneider chases the phantom over a cliff. "No one of all the simple population knew how eagerly and joyously he had found his lost mate." [286]

This depressing story does have its rough moments. The steady, dreary chronicle is too often interrupted with the familiar Dreiserian asides, especially forced commentaries on the simple nature of his protagonists. And at times Dreiser, the pseudo-scientist, interrupts: "That particular lull that comes in the systole-diastole of this earthly ball at two o'clock in the morning." [284] But the story is successful, combining a lyric quality epitomized in the title and the descriptions of the landscape, with the hard facts of farm life.

They had lived here, these two, ever since their marriage, forty-eight years before, and Henry had lived here before that from his childhood up. His father and mother, well along in years when he was a boy, had invited him to bring his wife here when he had first fallen in love and decided to marry; and he had done so. . . . Of the seven children, all told, that had been born to them, three had died; one girl had gone to Kansas; one boy had gone to Sioux Falls, never even to be heard of after; another boy had gone to Washington; and the last girl lived five counties away in the same State, but was so burdened with cares of her own that she rarely gave them a thought. Time and a commonplace home life that had never been attractive had weaned them thoroughly, so that, wherever they were, they gave little thought as to how it might be with their father and mother. [272–73]

The petty details of farm life are noted, and the minor quarrels of the elderly couple are presented in some detail. F. O. Matthiessen is quite correct in calling this Dreiser's most poetic story,[8] yet it is the artful juxtaposition of the dreary, daily existence with the later mystic quality of the search that makes the tale so successful. We feel we are face to face with pain and truth, just as we were with "Nigger Jeff," and this is truth given us by an accomplished artist. As Sherwood Anderson noted, "If there is a modern movement in American prose writing, a movement toward greater courage and fidelity in writing, then Theodore Dreiser is the pioneer and the hero of the movement." [9]

ii

My study, while facing some of the critical questions which inevitably arise in any discussion of Dreiser's work, deals, for the most part, with the themes present in his novels. There are, however, some qualities evident in all his books, qualities of spirit rather than tone, subject, or artistry. Man's courage in the face of tragedy, the bitterness, the sadness of

America is usually at the heart of most of his fiction. Such an attitude towards life, of course, could slop over into a maudlin sentimentality if it were not for Dreiser's sense of wonder, his sympathy for and amazement at the way his characters operate, and survive. In this he is close to Faulkner. There is an energy and fierce sense of purpose common to both novelists.

I have concentrated on Dreiser's novels, but he was also the prolific author of poetry, plays, short stories, and nonfiction. The less said about his poetry and drama, the better. Dreiser simply wasn't a poet or dramatist. His shorter works of fiction contain many of the attributes of his novels, though very few come close to *An American Tragedy* or *The Bulwark*. Dreiser needed a large canvas. His nonfiction, especially his autobiographical works, have never been adequately dealt with, and I believe it is in this area that new studies of Dreiser will be most needed. The University of Pennsylvania recently issued an edition of Dreiser's collected letters, and this material will undoubtedly focus attention on biographical matters. *Dawn*, Dreiser's account of his early life, especially deserves revival and re-evaluation.

In the field of his novels most of the criticism has been in the nature of violent attacks or spirited defenses. As Dreiser comes to be an accepted part of American literary history, however, there will be more scholarly and critical, and less polemical, attention paid to his work. Indeed, such a trend is already established; we have begun to assess and appreciate the various aspects of Dreiser's achievement as a novelist.

And this achievement, I believe, marks him as one of our best novelists, a rare man who was able to make art out of his vision of life. Admittedly, Dreiser still bothers many readers. Perhaps Alfred Kazin is right when he observes that we often don't know how to react to Dreiser because a sense of contemplative-ness, wonder, and reverence is at the center of Drei-ser's world: "It is this lack of smartness, this puzzled lovingness for the substance of all our mystery, that explains why we do not know what to *do* with Dreiser today." [10]

But this refers to emotive reactions which are qualified by the time in which we live. If we often are unable to know how to handle our reactions to Dreiser, we can certainly appreciate these important chronicles of our American experience. For as Randolph Bourne said of Dreiser, "his faults are those of his material and of uncouth bulk, and not of shoddiness. He ex-presses an America that is in process of forming. The interest he evokes is part of the eager interest we feel in that growth." [11]

NOTES

1—*Sister Carrie and Jennie Gerhardt*

1. Sinclair Lewis, "Nobel Prize Speech of 1930," *Appreciation of Lewis and Address by Lewis Before the Swedish Academy* (New York, 1930).

2. Ralph Waldo Emerson, "Ode, Inscribed to W. H. Channing," *Ralph Waldo Emerson*, ed. Frederic J. Carpenter (New York, 1934), p. 392.

3. Francis Fergusson, *Idea of the Theatre* (Princeton, 1949), p. 230.

4. Theodore Dreiser, *Sister Carrie* (New York: Boni and Liveright, 1917), pp. 48–50. Subsequent references—in the text—are to this edition.

5. Theodore Dreiser, *The Color of a Great City* (New York: H. Liveright, 1923), pp. 85–99.

6. Arthur Miller, *Death of a Salesman* (New York, 1949), p. 138.

7. *The Color of a Great City*, p. 266.

8. Theodore Dreiser, *Dawn* (New York: H. Liveright, 1931), pp. 9, 12.

9. F. O. Matthiessen, *Theodore Dreiser* (New York, 1951), p. 4.

10. Theodore Dreiser, *Jennie Gerhardt* (New York: World Publishing Co., 1946), p. 1. Subsequent references in the text are to this edition.

11. David Riesman, *The Lonely Crowd* (New Haven, 1950), p. 57.

2—The Financier, The Titan, The Stoic

1. Helen Dreiser, *My Life With Dreiser* (New York, 1951), pp. 123–24.

2. Charles Child Walcutt, *American Naturalism: A Divided Stream* (Minneapolis, 1956), p. 200.

3. Theodore Dreiser, *The Stoic* (New York: Doubleday, 1947), pp. 187–88. Copyright 1947 by Helen Dreiser. Quoted by permission of Doubleday & Co., Inc., and the trustees of the Dreiser Trust. Subsequent references in the text are to this edition.

4. Herbert Gold, "The Age of Happy Problems," in *Atlantic* (March, 1957), p. 58.

5. Stuart P. Sherman, "The Barbaric Naturalism of Mr. Dreiser," *The Nation* (Dec. 2, 1915) reprinted in *The Stature of Theodore Dreiser*, eds. Alfred Kazin and Charles Shapiro (Bloomington, 1955), p. 78.

6. Alfred Kazin, *On Native Grounds* (New York, 1942), pp. 86–87.

7. F. O. Matthiessen, *Dreiser*, p. 132.

8. Dreiser, *The Financier* (New York: Harper & Bros., 1912), p. 735. Subsequent references in the text are to this edition.

9. Thomas Whipple, "Aspects of a Pathfinder," in *Stature of Dreiser*, p. 99.

10. Ludwig Lewisohn, "An American Memory," in *Stature of Dreiser*, p. 18.

11. *Ibid.*

12. Eliseo Vivas, "Dreiser, An Inconsistent Mechanist," in *Stature of Dreiser*, p. 242.

13. Theodore Dreiser, *The Titan* (New York: John Lane, 1914), p. 399.

14. Ford Madox Ford, "Portrait of Dreiser," in *Stature of Dreiser*, p. 24.

15. See James T. Farrell, "Some Correspondence With Theodore Dreiser," in Kazin and Shapiro, *Stature of Dreiser*, pp. 36–50.

3—The "Genius"

1. Theodore Dreiser, The "Genius" (New York: H. Liveright, 1923), p. 9. Subsequent references in the text are to this edition.

2. Robert Spiller, The Cycle of American Literature (New York, 1955), p. 238.

3. Helen Dreiser, My Life With Dreiser (New York, 1951), p. 81.

4. Matthiessen, Dreiser, p. 159.

5. Leslie Katz, Review of "William Glackens and the Ashcan Group" by Ira Glackens, Arts, XXXII (February, 1958), 15.

6. Joseph Kwiat, "Dreiser's The 'Genius' and Everett Shinn, the Ash Can Painter," PMLA, LXVII (March, 1952), 31.

7. Robert M. Coates, "Fifty Years After," The New Yorker, XXXIII (February 15, 1958), 78.

8. David Brion Davis, "Dreiser and Naturalism Revisited," in Stature of Dreiser, p. 230.

9. Joseph Kwiat, "Dreiser and the Graphic Artist," American Quarterly, XXX (Summer, 1951), 127-41.

10. Robert Elias, Theodore Dreiser: Apostle of Nature (New York, 1949), p. 155.

11. Burton Roscoe, Theodore Dreiser (New York, 1925), p. 57.

12. Saul Bellow, The Adventures of Augie March (New York, 1953), p. 120.

13. Elias, Dreiser: Apostle of Nature, p. 195.

14. Randolph Bourne, "Desire as Hero," The New Republic, V (November 20, 1915), 5-6.

15. Henry James, The Princess Casamassima (New York, 1908), I, 84, 163.

16. Ibid., pp. xxii-xxiii.

17. Matthiessen, Dreiser, p. 166.

18. Norman Mailer, Barbary Shore (New York, 1953), p. 174.

19. H. L. Mencken, "The Dreiser Bugaboo," in *Stature of Dreiser*, p. 90.

20. H. L. Duffus, "Dreiser," *The American Mercury*, VII (January, 1926), 73.

4—The Bulwark

1. Theodore Dreiser, *The Bulwark* (New York: Doubleday, 1946), pp. v–vi. Copyright 1946 by Doubleday & Co., Inc. Quoted by permission of the publisher and the Dreiser Trust. Subsequent references in the text are to this edition.

2. Elias, *Dreiser: Apostle of Nature*, p. 300.

3. Granville Hicks, "Theodore Dreiser and 'The Bulwark' " in *Stature of Dreiser*, p. 220.

4. Edmund Wilson, "Theodore Dreiser's Quaker and Graham Greene's Priest," *The New Yorker*, XXII (March 23, 1946), 88.

5. Mason Wade, Review of *The Bulwark*, *Commonweal*, XLIV (June 14, 1946), 220.

6. Matthiessen, *Dreiser*, pp. 242–43.

7. Unpublished letter, Terence Martin (1958).

8. Ludwig Lewisohn, *Expression in America* (New York, 1932), p. 478.

9. Wilson, *New Yorker* (March 23, 1946), p. 91.

10. Hicks, in *Stature of Dreiser*, p. 220.

11. Harry M. Campbell, "A New Dreiser," *Western Review*, XI (Winter, 1947), 106.

12. Percy Lubbock, *The Craft of Fiction* (New York, 1957), p. 230.

13. Hicks, in *Stature of Dreiser*, p. 222.

14. Helen Dreiser, *My Life With Dreiser*, p. 289.

15. Elias, *Dreiser: Apostle of Nature*, p. 300.

16. Farrell, in *Stature of Theodore Dreiser*, pp. 45, 47.

17. Hicks, in *Stature of Dreiser*, p. 224.

5—An American Tragedy

1. J. Donald Adams, "Speaking of Books," *New York Times Book Review*, February 16 and April 6, 1958.

2. Randall Stewart, "Dreiser and the Naturalistic Heresy," *Virginia Quarterly Review*, XXXIV (Winter, 1958), 105–16.

3. Robert Shafer, "*An American Tragedy*: A Humanistic Demurrer," in *Stature of Dreiser*, p. 121, 124.

4. *N. Y. Times Book Review*, April 6, 1958.

5. William Lyon Phelps, "As I Like It," *Scribner's Magazine*, LXXIV (April, 1926), 433–34.

6. H. L. Mencken, introduction to *An American Tragedy* (New York, 1948), p. 8.

7. Matthiessen, *Dreiser*, p. 198.

8. Theodore Dreiser, *An American Tragedy* (New York: World Publishing Co., 1948), p. 348. Subsequent references in the text are to this edition.

9. John Berryman, "Dreiser's Imagination," in *Stature of Dreiser*, p. 152.

10. Matthiessen, *Dreiser*, p. 203.

11. Helen Dreiser, *My Life With Dreiser*, pp. 71–72, 76.

12. The Detroit *News*, March 30, 1958, p. 4A.

13. Elias, *Dreiser: Apostle of Nature*, pp. 218–19.

14. Helen Dreiser, *My Life With Dreiser*, p. 163.

15. Elias, *Dreiser: Apostle of Nature*, p. 238.

16. Matthiessen, *Dreiser*, pp. 190, 196.

17. Randolph Bourne, "The Art of Theodore Dreiser," in *Stature of Dreiser*, p. 95.

18. Joseph Warren Beach, *The Twentieth Century Novel* (New York, 1932), pp. 323–24.

19. Shafer, in *Stature of Dreiser*, p. 122.

20. John Chamberlain, "Theodore Dreiser Remembered," in *Stature of Dreiser*, p. 131.

21. Matthiessen, *Dreiser*, pp. 194, 206.

22. *Ibid.*, pp. 11–12, 169.

6—The Short Stories

1. The edition used is *The Best Short Stories of Theodore Dreiser*, ed. by Howard Fast (New York: World Publishing Co., 1947), p. 68.

2. Most references will be to the three stories discussed

in detail, but horrendous examples can be culled from such stories as "A Doer of the Word," "Convention," and "St. Columba and the River."

3. James T. Farrell, Introduction to *The Best Short Stories of Theodore Dreiser* (New York: Premier Edition, 1961), p. vii.

4. *Best Short Stories*, p. 8.

5. Sherwood Anderson, Introduction to *Free and Other Stories* (New York, 1918), p. v.

6. Elias, *Dreiser: Apostle of Nature*, p. 209.

7. Robert Elias, ed., *Letters of Theodore Dreiser* (Philadelphia, 1959), p. 177.

8. Matthiessen, *Dreiser*, p. 181.

9. Anderson, *Free*, p. vi.

10. Alfred Kazin, "Introduction," *Stature of Dreiser*, p. 11.

11. Randolph Bourne, in *Stature of Dreiser*, p. 95.

INDEX